WAKE UP AMERICA

Pastor Bic -
We appreciate you +
your family.

Gods Bless -

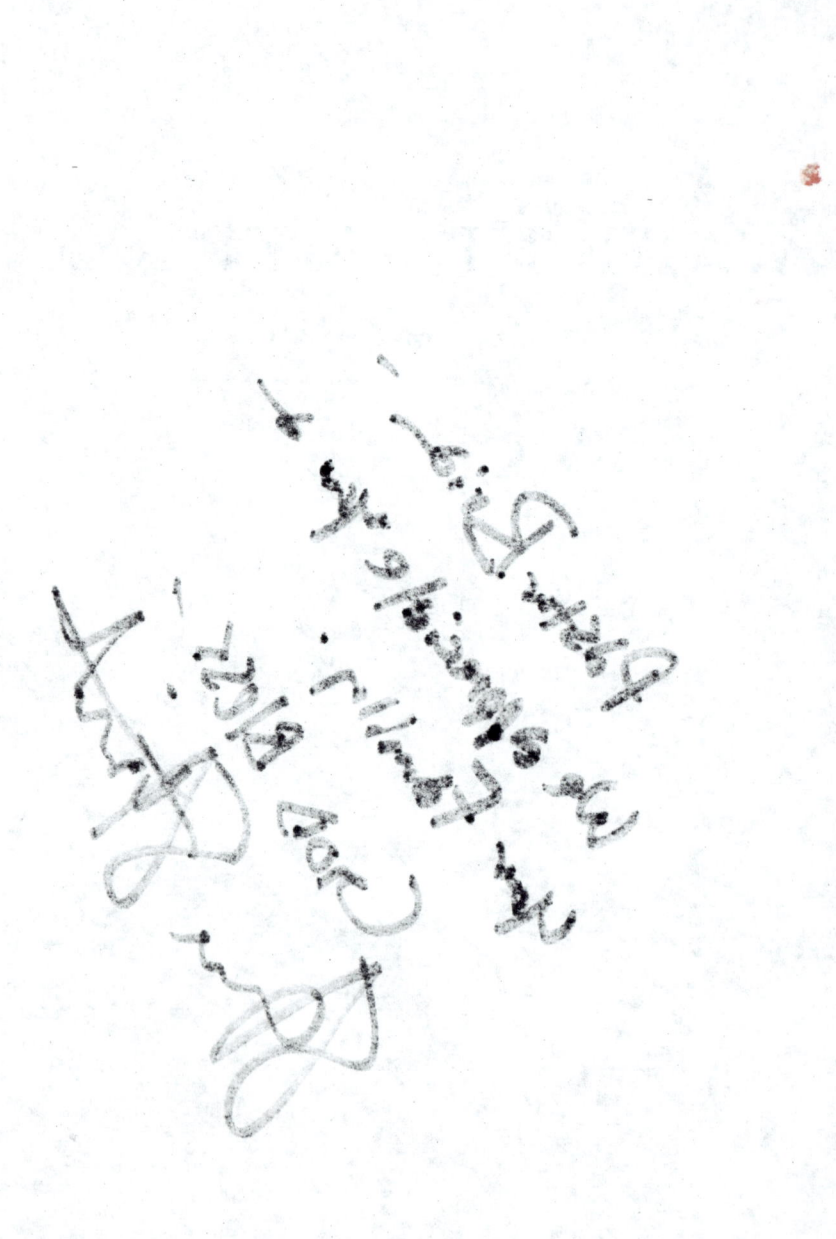

WAKE UP AMERICA

A VISION OF SPIRITUAL APATHY

STEVE STRICKLAND

Tate Publishing & *Enterprises*

Published by Tate Publishing & Enterprises, LLC
127 E. Trade Center Terrace | Mustang, Oklahoma 73064 USA
1.888.361.9473 | www.tatepublishing.com

Tate Publishing is committed to excellence in the publishing industry. The company reflects the philosophy established by the founders, based on Psalms 68:11,
"The Lord gave the word and great was the company of those who published it."

Book design copyright © 2007 by Tate Publishing, LLC. All rights reserved.
Cover design by Genevieve E. Stolter
Interior design by Jennifer L. Fisher

Published in the United States of America

ISBN: 978-1-60247-809-1
1. Adult nonfiction   2. Christian, Morals and Ethics
07.08.03

This book is dedicated to my entire family, but specifically my wife, Diane. What an incredible woman to have stood by me through all the highs and lows of life. Despite all my flaws, she believes in me. She loves me unconditionally, which is more than I could ever ask of her. To my four children, Megan, Makayla, Jacob, Justin; who at times were more excited about me writing this book than *I* was to write it! They all hold me accountable. I know they look up to me as an example of what a Christ follower should be. They will largely form their opinions about who God is and what it means to be a Christ follower by observing my actions! Nothing I could write could thank all of them enough for their love and support.

TABLE OF CONTENTS

PREFACE

It was a dream of mine to write a book before I ever formally entered the ministry. That dream was soon to be cast on to the back-burner of life and all but forgotten! There was full-time secular work, full-time volunteer ministry as a youth pastor and worship leader, a family of six and evenings of secluded study in order to meet the requirements for my ministry credentials. I had literally forgotten about the opportunity God had made evident that He was going to provide for me to write. It was just about one month ago that I was on a prayer retreat by myself. It was during that time when God miraculously revived that dream. I shared my dreams with my wife and God continued to confirm that it was time to start writing.

Not long after and just before I had begun writing, my wife called me one day at work to encourage me. She read to me from her journal entry she had written about ten months earlier. It contained some details about our recent resignation and the difficult times we were in the midst of. Later, in the same journal entry, she described in detail about how I had woken in the middle of the night with some ideas for a message titled, "I have a dream." It was not by coincidence that when we arrived in church the next Sunday, we listened to a message titled, "Dreams Never Die." God was really trying to get my attention. Maybe you are like me in that it seems you need Him to really whack you upside the head in order to get a picture of what He is saying to you. In my little world, there was a lot happening that all pointed to the same thing, simply reminding us of what we really already knew!

In spite of all the prompting, I still felt extremely unworthy. Not inadequate, unwilling or unable; but unworthy. The Bible describes Noah as meek and Moses as humble. I'm not exactly sure if those are the same as feeling unworthy, but it is the feeling that seems to often encapsulate how I feel. Paul described himself in his writing to Timothy as the chief amongst sinners and I often know how he feels. There are so many people out there that God could choose to use. I don't know why God has chosen to use me to minister to others or why He will choose to use me in the future. I do know that God will often choose to use men and women here on earth to accomplish His will and purpose. He certainly does not have to, but more often than not, that is the means He uses.

I do know this: in order to be effectively used by God, you must remain humble and broken before Him. You must maintain purity in life, thoughts and actions. You must be eager and willing to learn. You must never be so prideful as to think you have learned enough. You must be willing to be content if you are never used by God again; but then pray fervently that He *will* use you again. This concept is one of the life lessons God has shown me during our recent time of transition in ministry. There was a distinct and divine call for us to leave where we were. We didn't have anywhere to go. We hadn't secretly planned our resignation after securing a new position somewhere else. We didn't know where we were going to go or what we were going to do. We were comfortable where we were. Our church was really the only church our children had ever known. There were a lot of questions, but we simply knew that the first step we had to take was to leave where we were. So, that is exactly what we did.

That was a very difficult step, one that forced me to my knees in order to try and gain direction and guidance for what was next. On one specific occasion during that time of seeking direction, I was confronted with a most unusual question. It haunted me for several days before I even had the courage to try and acknowledge it. That one pressing question I continually felt coming to the forefront of my thoughts was in the form of a question God was asking me. The question was this: "Steve, would you be satisfied if I chose to never use you again?"

Wow! Think about that for a second. I can honestly say that I thought about it for more than a second. It's a question that requires a simple yes or no response. Sounds easy enough, right? After all, I have a fifty-percent chance of getting it right! What I didn't realize at the time was this: there is no wrong answer to that question, just wrong attitudes behind your answer.

I tossed around the reasons for answering yes, and then pondered the reasons to answer no. Ultimately, I started to get really agitated and frustrated and in a moment of heated prayer with God I gave Him my answer. It was an emphatic, "No way!" My reasons were simple. I was willing, able and trained to do the work of the ministry. Why in the world would God even ask me such a thing as this? It has always been the desire of both my wife and I to be in the ministry full-time. Doesn't the Bible say that He would give us the desires of our heart? I continued to justify my response for quite some time, but time would not stop the probing question from constantly being thrown in my face whenever I started to engage God in some way. I even tried changing my answer, thinking that would give me some relief from what had really become a nagging annoyance in my life.

After wrestling with this question for some time, the message that was reverberating just beneath the surface of the question found its way out of my head and finally penetrated my heart. At that moment of realization, *my* will was broken. I was suddenly able to be thankful for what God has already done for me, in me and through me. I found myself somewhere I never thought I would be. I no longer needed to do what I thought I should do. I became willing to do (or not do) whatever God wanted. I no longer needed things to happen according to my timeline, but was willing to serve and grow where I was until God directed me further.

Abraham had to choose to lay his son on the altar to be sacrificed. It wasn't until he made that choice and took action toward following through on it that God provided a substitution for the sacrifice. In turn, it wasn't until I laid aside my will, desire and expectations in a broken state of prayer and intercession that God was even able to step in and give direction as to what He wanted us to do! Don't get me wrong, this journey has been anything but easy, even after that epiphany. So often, we let our pride become a hindrance to our walk with the Lord. Fortunately, God is gracious, merciful and even more amazing; much more than you or I could ever ask, think or imagine.

INTRODUCTION

Being in the ministry is a very humbling place. The weight of responsibility to those looking to you for spiritual guidance is immense. The overwhelming burden to constantly deliver a word from God that is not only accurate, but in season can be enough to push you to the brink of retirement, every week! Each time I stand behind a pulpit or lectern, it is a constant reminder of my own humanity and frailty. Having said all of that, I hope you will better understand why the experience that developed into the initial outline for this book is so difficult to communicate. Maybe you will further grasp why it took so long from the initial event in 1999 to get to the form in which you read it now. It was in July of 1999 that God chose to communicate a message of spiritual apathy to me that I will communicate in the pages of this book. The message came by way of a vision that metaphorically describes the state of the 21st century American Church.

When Jesus taught by parable, His message was often directed to a very specific group of people. There was always, however, a message for the larger audience at hand as well. Jesus spoke to teach, so He spoke in simple terms and with simple stories. Even His most simple messages were often constructed with layers of lessons and teaching to be absorbed by the hearers, both immediately and after further contemplation. Many of the obvious aspects were discovered and applied right away. Other aspects of the message and application of the message became clearer later, after certain life experiences, reflection and introspection. Even the writers of the New Testament often indicated they were present and heard what Jesus was teaching, but really didn't understand the depth of meaning or application until later.

In the same way, what happened to me involved layers of lessons and insight. Some of those layers have become clearer over time. I am sure there are others that are still yet to be understood. Since it happened, God has used this experience to teach me things. At times, things that may have normally been overlooked in my life have become life lessons or have evolved into personal teaching moments. It has been through these series of lessons that I have come to feel the need to share and communicate with others. The pages that follow are intended to draw your attention to things. Some of them will be obvious right away; some of them may require further reflection and introspection.

In our society today, there is so much competing for your attention, interest, and ultimately for your very soul. All of these things work to distract you from your relationship with God through Jesus Christ. The simple truth is this: most American's would categorize themselves as "Christian." I've conducted informal studies on more than one occasion that support this. If you were to go to any public location today and survey one-hundred people, upwards of seventy percent or more of those people would label themselves that way. Let's look at some more scientific research. The Barna Research Group found that of those claiming to be a born again Christian, forty percent did not bother to share their faith in Jesus Christ with a non-believer. Even more alarming is that of that forty-percent above, only fifty-seven percent believe the Bible is totally accurate in all of its teachings. Only thirty-eight percent claim to have a personal responsibility to share their religious beliefs. A mere twenty-six percent believe that Satan is anything more than just a symbolism of evil. Only forty-five percent said Jesus did not sin during His time on earth. Thirty-six percent believe public schools should teach creationism. [1]

The responses above are from people that consider themselves to be born again Christians. Barna went further to classify this group as people who said they have "made a personal commitment to Jesus Christ that is still important in their life today. This group also believes that when they die they will go to heaven because they had confessed their sins and had accepted Jesus Christ as their savior!"

If this is the mindset of America at large, is it not fairly easy to understand why our country is in the position it is in? There is a simple common-sense aphorism attributed to Albert Einstein that says, "Insanity is doing the same thing over and over again expecting different results." As you prepare to read this book, my prayer is simple. Do not just nod your head in agreement with the words on the page and then go about your life doing the same things you have always done; that would be insane.

Take special notice of the last chapter, "*Taking Action.*" It is designed to give you some practical helps and ideas on how to wake up the 21ˢᵗ century Christian, starting with you.

THE VISION

My experience began as I was sitting at work on Monday July 12th, 1999. It was just like any other ordinary day at the office. I was consumed with the normal activities of the day when lunch time arrived. I needed to do some reading and studying in order to finish preparing my message for the youth service I would be preaching two days later. I opened my Bible to and began to read Colossians 3:1–17. I had read the same section of scripture a hundred times, but this time, on this particular day, it was going to be very different.

After reading, I closed my eyes and began to meditate on the words I had just read. All of a sudden, I was transported in my mind's eye to an open area where there were swarms of people as far as the eye could see in all directions. It was as vivid an experience as I have ever had. I did not feel as though I was dreaming; it was as though I was actually being physically transported into this place where I now found myself. I was not placed amongst the people, but rather felt as though I was being suspended above them. I was able to get close enough to hear that conversations were taking place, but not close enough to engage the people or actually discern what they were saying.

Amongst the sea of people, my eyes were drawn to a large white object amongst the myriad of colors. Once this object caught my attention, I was taken closer and closer until I was suspended about ten feet above it. As I got closer and the white object became more visible, I figured out what it was. Right there, right in the middle of all the hustle and bustle of the people, was a hospital gurney with a man lying in it. Without hearing a word, my intuition told me that the man lying on the bed was either asleep or in some sort of unconscious state. As obvious as it was that the man was unable to communicate, I had a very strong sense that he was aware of his surroundings and able to understand what was going on around him. Even more than the sense of awareness that I felt, it seemed I was able to sense what the man was feeling. It was an internal urging, a desire to sit up. He wanted to get out of bed and get involved in the activity around him. Unfortunately, he was too weak to do so.

After all the intense focus and seeming connection with the man on the gurney, my attention was drawn to a man standing directly behind the front, or head section, of the gurney. As I studied the form and features of this man, I had a sickening feeling in the pit of my stomach. I realized something very bizarre that was both shocking and confusing. The man lying in the gurney and the man standing directly at the front of it was the same man. The man standing was carrying on a conversation with someone else. He was alive, vibrant and free to move around and communicate with anyone else. I could sense, however, that this man had no awareness of the hospital gurney or the man on it. In fact, I had a sense that no one amongst the crowd was even remotely aware of the gurney or a man lying on it.

THE LAST DAYS

Just like that, as suddenly as it started, it was over. While it seemed like a significant amount of time had passed, it lasted about as long as it takes to warm up a cup of coffee in the microwave.

The images and sensations from that vision were burned into my mind. I could think of nothing else at the time. In fact, I often still see some those images when I close my eyes to meditate.

After it was over, I was full of emotion. The scale tipped all the way from euphoric to distressing. I wanted to understand what this was all about, but in some aspects was intimidated by what had just happened. As I contemplated and prayed about it, my first thoughts were to the scripture Peter quoted from Joel 2 as he preached on the day of Pentecost in the second chapter of Acts. That text says, "In the last days, God said, I will pour out my Spirit upon all people. Your sons and daughters will prophesy, your young men will see visions, and your old men will dream dreams" (Acts 2:17, NLT).

It is quite evident to me, when matching up the Word of God with current events, that we are living in the era that will likely see the second coming of our Lord Jesus Christ. These are the last days! The verse referred to a pouring out of His Spirit and we see His outpouring all around the world in the form of revivals, miracles, signs and wonders. The verse also mentioned young men seeing visions and since I was a mere thirty-one at the time, I began to believe the experience was meant to serve as a warning of some kind.

READY OR NOT, HERE IT COMES

Over the next few days, the images I saw preoccupied my every moment. I needed to know why me. I had to understand what it was all about. I wanted to get serious about trying to understand. It was on the third day after it happened that I returned to where I was reading when it all started. I was reading from Colossians 3:1–17. So, I began to read it again. I read it again, and again, and again. As I read it for about the fifth time in a row, I began to see certain flashes of the images from the vision as I read. The message behind the vision began to line up with the text in Colossians and the characters in the vision began to come alive as principles of the text. Some of the big ideas that became apparent to me from the vision were:

- The person lying on the gurney is a representation of the spiritual life in the church of America at large today

- The person standing at the head of the gurney is a representation of the carnal life of the church of America at large today

- By disengaging our spirit man, we allow contentment to replace revival

- God is desirous to use us but we remain satisfied being unused

WAKE UP

You may have heard of the expression, "breaking up is hard to do." As I get older, I find waking up much harder to do. Not necessarily because I need more sleep, or even that I am not getting enough sleep. I just find it harder to get things going in the morning once I roll out of bed! Ordinary tasks, like actually getting out of bed, seem to become more difficult as we grow older.

It is crucial as a Christian to understand that we need to constantly be awake. Of course, this does not refer to a physical sense, but rather a spiritual sense. As Christians, we must be fully engaged and aware of our surroundings. As real as the physical things in our lives are, there is a spiritual side to our lives that often is overlooked, even by Christians. The cosmic battle between good and evil, depicted in almost every science fiction movie known to man, is actually reality. That spiritual battle begins the moment anyone decides to turn their life over to God by trusting in Jesus Christ as their Lord and Savior. At that moment, the Christian is empowered by God to live a righteous life and make wise choices. Of course, that's when the enemy also starts his bidding for our soul. He presents us with temptation that, if acted upon, would take us off target in a spiritual sense and send us down the same road the majority seems to favor. It is really easy to write off the invisible side of our spiritual life instead of remaining aware of it. Being aware of this fact is the first step to waking up, spiritually speaking.

Everyone in the world has some basic needs. God has promised to provide for our needs. The spiritual battle begins when we are tempted regarding this in one of two ways. First, we may be tempted to deny the fact that God actually will provide for our needs. This is a lie. Of course, it won't be presented in the context of a lie. Rather, it will be dressed up as both a logical and rational explanation. The second method would be to manipulate your perception of a desire to be equal to a legitimate need. This means that something not classifiable as a need would take on that very definition in our mind. Just because we have come to believe it to be true, does not make it true. You may want a new car, but you also may not actually need one. It would be nice to have, it would be more convenient, more accommodating, more exciting, but none of that makes it necessary.

Please do not think I am saying Christians can not have a new car or desire nice things. These types of issues always boil down to a matter of the desires and intentions of your heart. If you stay aware and mindful of your constant spiritual battle, your heart is more likely to remain pure. Maintaining this awareness will allow you to desire things with a bigger picture in mind. The bigger picture will allow you to maintain pure motives and intentions, which will speak volumes for your hearts condition. Spiritually speaking, when you are operating in this capacity, you are alert and awake. Understanding your heart is something that God does better than anyone. In life, you will encounter plenty of people that will claim to know your thoughts, your motives and even try to judge your intentions. Ignore those people and listen to God, the only one who really knows and the only one that really matters.

All too often, action and activity is confused with intention.

We become consumed with doing what we think is the right thing, regardless of our intention. A perfect example would be the general "Christian" opinion about money. An often misquoted section of scripture says that money is the root of all evil. In fact, the scripture indicates it is the love of money that was and always will be inherently evil. It always boils down to the desire and intentions of the heart rather than the object or action itself.

The underlying intention of why we do what we do is the key to spiritual alertness. When you wake up to your true intentions, you learn a lot about where your heart is. Meet Jim, a young man that has been raised in the church his entire life. Jim attends church all the time, engages in worship and hangs out with other young people from his church. Jim is a good kid, but does almost everything he does because of the influence of his parents. Jim knows exactly how to act and what to say in order to keep his parent's off his back. He knows how to answer the questions that are asked of him because he knows what his parents want to hear. Jim's activity says one thing, but his intentions say something totally different. Jim is spiritually asleep, despite his involvement in church and activity with other Christian friends. Jim is asleep because he's trying to please his parents and stay in their good graces rather than develop his relationship with God. While a good relationship between parent and child is important, it pales in comparison to a personal relationship with God through Jesus Christ. That relationship must be everyone's primary focus.

This seems so obvious, but it is the *obvious* that is often easily overlooked. Your spirit needs to be alert, alive and awake. Paul said in Colossians that we "have been raised with Christ." It is a privilege to be raised with Christ. We have all the benefits that come with the resurrection of Christ. Power over sin, victory over death, eternal life with God in heaven... the list goes on and on.

In nature, a caterpillar goes through a transforming process known as metamorphosis. If the caterpillar never entered the cocoon, it could never become what it was created to be; a butterfly. Christians must also go through a transformation process. The transformation from the old to the new self is described by Paul in his letter to the church at Ephesus:

> "Once you were dead; doomed forever because of your many sins. You used to live just like the rest of the world, full of sin, obeying Satan, the mighty prince of the power of the air. He is the spirit at work in the hearts of those who refuse to obey God. All of us used to live that way, following the passions and desires of our evil nature. We were born with an evil nature, and we were under God's anger just like everyone else. But God is so rich in mercy, and He loved us so very much, that even while we were dead because of our sins, He gave us life when He raised Christ from the dead. (It is only by God's special favor that you have been saved!) For He raised us from the dead along with Christ, and we are seated with Him in the heavenly realms—all because we are one with Christ Jesus."

(Ephesians 2:1–6, NLT)

When a man gets married, he embarks on a new life. At almost every corner there is an opportunity to meet a variety of changes, challenges, and choices. There is no change that's as invasive and comprehensive as the change that takes place when someone commits their life to Christ.

I've seen so many times that a new Christian becomes surprised when, after the initial emotional high of committing their lives to Christ has worn off a little, they begin to struggle to live out that new life. I'm not sure why it is a surprise, but it happens very frequently. It is as though they expected everything to be fresh, new, and wonderful forever! They expected to live a life free from pain, struggle, worry, or defeat. The fact is we all have to live with some measure of hurt and disappointment. This may seem discouraging. However, it teaches a very valuable lesson: the power to be dominated by the sinful nature or to be led by the Spirit lies within man's free will. In fact, life is, in its simplest form, just a series of choices. When the easy choice becomes a little more difficult over time, it all boils down to a choice to do what is right in spite of your feelings or to do what is wrong because of your feelings.

Paul certainly is qualified to speak about choices and a transformed life. He went from persecutor to preacher, from murderer to missionary. When he woke up to his need for a Savior, he made the choice to make a commitment to Him. His life got pretty complicated after that. He was beat up and beat down. He was whipped and stoned. He was shipwrecked and homeless. He was destitute and naked. Sure, there were some good times too, but Paul's life reads like a tale from the dark side after his experience on the road to Damascus. Many people make the initial choice to commit, but then forget about the need to continue to make the same choice day in and day out.

CAR SHOPPING

If I were to take you out to look for a car, you would naturally be drawn to a car that looks fun, exciting and appeals to your taste. It may very well be your favorite color or have a feature that has always been something you have wanted in a car. After salivating over the car of your dreams, if I tried to convince you to take a serious look at a rust-bucket, useless piece of junk on the corner of the lot that may or may not make the trip to your home, you'd likely tell me to get lost. It's usually pretty easy to say no to the "ugly" option.

Let's now assume that I took you by a very ordinary car, without many of the exciting features. It's very likely you would still be looking back over your shoulder at the flashy, trendy, exciting car of your dreams. Despite the long term benefits like better gas mileage, efficiency, practicality and lower price, there would likely be an impulsive or instinctive desire for the attractive and exciting features of the other car. Temptation will come roaring into your life, all four wheels squealing. The engine will be tuned to perfection and the body will be glossy, right off the showroom floor. If temptation arrived in the form of a rusted-out 1972 Gremlin, none of us would even take a second look.

The danger in most temptation is the lie that says it won't cost you anything. The consequences won't be immediately visible. It is amazing to me that everyday-people give into temptations that could ruin their career, marriage and family, all for a little pleasure or enjoyment for a few moments. To put it plainly, the enemy's plan is to distract you by offering you *attractive* things. Your weaknesses, and we all have them, will be exploited to make the temptation that much more powerful. Once your focus is drawn to these things, you become distracted from the things of God. Once distracted, you no longer have a proper perspective. Once your perspective is skewed, it becomes easier to convince you that your situation and circumstances are special and God will understand. Once you begin to believe the lie, you are in big trouble.

When you buy into any of these schemes, you begin to feed the appetite and desire more. Meanwhile, your spirit man suffers from malnourishment on the sideline, trying to get your attention. When one flourishes, the other suffers. Temptations simply serve as a means to distract our attention away from God and onto ourselves.

BUBBLES

In a way, many Christians try to live their life as though they were chasing bubbles. You've probably been at a kid's party where all the little kids were running around with excitement on their face while chasing bubbles. It's amazing to me the amount of joy they show for what amounts to a really useless chase. Bubbles certainly are fun to make, they come in lots of shapes and sizes and practically anyone can make them. All bubbles have this one thing in common though; they eventually pop! Whether you try to hold a bubble, or just let it fly free, sooner or later it is going to burst. When we stop being awake and alert to spiritual things, the temptations of this world become a wand full of fascinating bubbles. There are alluring pictures of fun, romance, happiness and wealth. For a while, the picture may actually seem real. Sooner or later, just when you think you've finally gotten enough, had enough, or become enough to make life work the way you want it to, just when you thought you might be lifted above all the frustrations and difficulties of life, something will come along and cause your bubble to burst!

The first thing that happens when your spirit man starts to nod off is you start to live life on your own strength. You develop a sense that you can take on this thing called life all by yourself. Once started down this path, it won't be long until you are mired in a life of disappointment, disillusionment and mediocrity. We need to keep our mind aware, alert and awake to the things of God. It's interesting to point out how many Christians like to quote scriptures such as, "Set your mind on things above, not on things on the earth" (Colossians 3:2, NKJV). Unfortunately, they don't often consider the entire context of that verse. We certainly want to set our mind on the things of God and not the things of this world. In fact, without that type of proper positive outlook, you will be doomed to live a negative life. You will simply bounce from one negative experience to the next. The Apostle Paul said not to be "conformed to this world, but be transformed by the renewing of your mind" (Romans 12:2, NKJV). You have to be able to filter the junk, the doubt and the negativity of this world from your mind. You have to decisively fill your mind with the truth of God's Word. It takes strength of character to maintain a positive outlook during the difficulties of life. You must discipline your mind, setting it on the things that have eternal value. As important as all of this is, many chose to ignore the first verse of Colossians chapter 3 as they quote the second verse. Most don't want to see (or admit) that there is more than just your mind to worry about. The first verse again reiterates the need for new life metaphorically, indicating you have been raised with Christ. The next phrase gets to the root of where the issues always originate: the heart. We are told to set our hearts on the things above, where Christ is seated on the right hand of God.

FAKING IT

When you don't constantly maintain your focus and awareness, it becomes really easy to get distracted. The fact that your mind is not set on eternal things can easily be hidden from others. We constantly know what we should be doing, so in our mind we can set forth an image of who we think we should be by doing the things we have come to realize others expect of us. We can fake and pretend to have our mind set on Christ by walking out a life of religiosity. We make others painfully aware of our spiritual superiority by judging and condemning those that have not reached our level.

It's easy to fake your day-to-day activity and the words you speak. It is much more difficult to hide whatever it is that has become the affection of our heart. Your mind is one part of your spiritual being but your heart is the true barometer of who you really are. You may even be able to fake the intentions of your heart for a time, but doing so will wear you out emotionally, physically and spiritually. I don't know how you feel when you haven't had enough sleep and you are exhausted, but I am a total grouch! In this distracted state, your spiritual man begins to tire, due to both a lack of nourishment and lack of exercise. You could say your spiritual muscles begin to atrophy. There is not a whole lot you can do effectively while you are exhausted or malnourished! When you wake up from sleeping, it takes some time to be able to focus properly. You're not as sharp as you are once you're completely awake. The way you wake up, spiritually, is to get your eyes, your desires and your heart off this world and the things it has to offer. The primary focus of your eyes, your desires and your heart needs to be on those things that have eternal value, especially your relationship with Jesus Christ. God only offers good gifts for His children, and that fact should be motivation enough for us to desire those things. Imagine wearing yourself out to the degree mentioned above. It won't be long before your misery equates to impatience, which will easily boil over into your attitude and actions. Then you won't be able to fake it anymore.

The facts are simple. Before you're committed to a relationship with God through Jesus Christ as your savior, you could care less about what God wanted you to do. You did whatever you wanted to do, whatever felt good or whatever everyone else was doing. Once you were awakened to spiritual things, you were given the power and authority to overcome those old ways of thinking and living. Our primary focus is not to be on the things and pleasures of this world but rather focused on the things above.

I am always amazed at how well my life goes when my priorities and focus are aligned properly. My relationship with my wife, my kids and my co-workers seems entirely determined by my relationship with my Lord! When I fail to spend the quality time that is needed in order to cultivate my relationship with God, I sense continual frustration, a lack of patience and judgmental or critical attitudes within me. It doesn't take a rocket scientist to figure out those kinds of things do not go over real well with the people you have to deal with on a daily basis. When I regain my focus and put my eyes on Him first, all my other relationships seem to fall into proper alignment. Even a crisis at work will be resolved more quickly when my focus is where it needs to be. I've called my wife from work on several occasions while frustrated. Her first words to me most of the time are, "Have you prayed about it?" As embarrassing as it always is to admit to her and now to all of you, I often get distracted by the issues life has dealt me and lose sight of my primary focus.

There is only one that can bring resolution to all of life's issues: God! That is where your focus needs to be. How true His Word is when it tells us it is when you seek the Lord and delight in Him that you will receive the desires of your heart, and may I add, hear the answers to your prayers!

OPEN YOUR EYES

Opening your eyes is a process. Any process is a process because it takes time to get from one point to the next. This idea is seen in Colossians 3:10 with the phrase "which is being renewed." It has the implication that this renewal is supposed to be an ongoing process.

When you wake up in the morning, one of the first steps you take to wake up is opening your eyes. You would never be at your best during the day if you had your eyes closed! How would you drive? How would you work? How would you get anywhere? The same is true when it comes to spiritual things also. You have to open your eyes in order to be effective in what you're to do. You have to be alert and aware of what is going on around you. Because it is just one step in the process, most people don't wake up simply by opening their eyes, jumping out of bed and suddenly being able to operate at their best. Some of us take a little longer than others to *warm-up* to the idea of getting out of bed. Some require twenty minutes of snooze pressing, a shower and a cup of coffee before they even think about trying to function.

Even with your eyes open, there are still steps involved in order to properly adjust to your situation. Imagine you're walking around in your house or maybe even somewhere else less familiar. Then imagine someone turned off the lights. If you were smart, you would stop and wait for your eyes to adjust to the light and situation before you tried to get anywhere. If you're like me, you figure you know where everything is and you keep walking and end up bumping your head or stubbing your toe. Even with your eyes wide open, there will be times when you will have to patiently wait and adjust to what your situations and circumstances bring your way. God has a way of turning out the lights on us when we think we have figured out just how to get around on our own. It is as though He purposely re-arranged the furniture then turned out the lights just to make sure you stub your toe and He gets your attention!

If you ever made a trip to the ophthalmologist for an eye exam, the doctor likely dilated your pupils. This is so he can look into the deepest parts of you eye and get a much better view of your retina, optic nerve and vessels in the back of the eye. Even though this procedure is painless, it is quite annoying. After the doctor is done you are left unable to focus on things that are close to you. Seeing and focusing on objects further away during this process is not as difficult, but it's no piece of cake either. When your focus is blurred, you lose sight of the things around you. Sometimes the situation or circumstance causing blurred vision may seem insignificant and painless. Sometimes your blurred vision is not even your fault. Even with your eyes open, you must take care not to lose sight of your future when your present gets to be a little foggy.

THE PROCESS

The idea of being renewed is not a point in time for anyone that calls themselves a Christian. It is really a process that lasts a lifetime. There is a definite beginning to that journey (salvation) and a definite end as well (physical death). This new self that is never described as *was renewed, can be renewed* or *will be renewed.* It is typically referred to through a verb of present-perfect-progressive-tense. That means it expresses duration of an action that began in the past, has continued into the present, and will continue into the future. That is a perfect and poetic description of what the Christian life is all about. Your growth, understanding and maturity in Christ are without end, always to be progressing and moving in a forward direction.

The Australian coat of arms pictures two of that country's native animals: the emu and the kangaroo. It's not just because of their indigenous nature that those two animals appear on this national symbol. The animals were chosen because they share one characteristic that appealed to the Australian citizens. Both the emu and kangaroo can move only forward. They were actually not created to move backwards. The emu has a three-toed foot that causes it to fall when it tries to go backwards. The kangaroo is prevented from moving in reverse by its large tail.

It's no coincidence that the founders chose *Advance Australia* as their motto. Those who truly desire to follow Jesus must be, in a spiritual sense, like the emu and kangaroo. There is no turning back in the life of a Christian, only moving forward. There is no room in your future for your past. There is no going back to your old ways once you have begun the journey of a life changed by the miracle of salvation.

It may sound oversimplified, but it is common sense that bears repeating; in order to move forward you can't go backwards. You can not go back to the way things used to be in your life before you were saved. You may be wondering if I think you should be perfect… not a chance! I'd be the biggest hypocrite in the world if that was my expectation of you, since it is not even true in my own life. However, you must constantly remain awake and alert; eyes wide open to your life. You must constantly put your flesh to death. That will only happen when you spend time cultivating your relationship with God through Jesus Christ. It doesn't matter how much you have grown or how long you have been saved, you must be constantly moving forward in your relationship.

Growth is achieved in centimeters not inches, inches not feet and feet not miles. Everything worthwhile will take some good old-fashioned hard work, dedication, time and effort. When I first accepted Jesus as my personal savior, there were some really obvious issues in my life. I honestly thought to myself as I pondered the work that God was doing in my life: *This is amazing what God is doing! Once he finishes with these issues over the next month or so, I'm going to be perfect.* I didn't realize how far from the truth that statement actually was until years later. Of course, God did begin a good work in me, but He is still seeing it through, even today.

The big idea here is that you just can't allow yourself to ever be satisfied with where you are at spiritually. There are really only three options for your relationship with God once you figure things are "good enough." First, you can grow cold and distant in your relationship with God because, after all, you've arrived and don't really need Him anymore. The second option is to become religious and judgmental, piously look down on everyone else around you. The only other option is indifference, which creates a stale, stagnate or dry relationship that goes nowhere. The moment you become satisfied with today's success, it immediately becomes your greatest obstacle in moving forward tomorrow. That is because there is a natural tendency to relax after a victory and let your guard down. It is a natural inclination to want to stop and catch your breath after you've reached some pinnacle or milestone. After all, you've worked hard to get where you are and deserve a break. Whenever you make the decision to stop trying and just coast for awhile, you have actually already begun to move backward. None of us can allow complacency, we must stay hungry.

So, if you catch yourself looking in the rear-view mirror at what you've done and are satisfied with what you see, then you have not done enough today to draw your attention beyond yesterday. It takes your constant attention to stay hungry for more and never be satisfied with where you are in your spiritual journey.

THE BEAST WITHIN

From this experience, I have learned what I like to call the *feast or famine* principle. It is a really obvious principle, but not necessarily easy or obvious to spot in your own life. It requires that you allow the Holy Spirit to look deep inside you. It requires that you begin to recognize what He wants you to see. It requires that you be totally honest and sincere in recognizing areas of your life that really do require your attention. The Holy Spirit will show you where you need work. It will be something you have to come to understand as you develop your relationship with God through Jesus Christ. You will begin to know and sense improper thoughts or attitudes that are still alive in you.

In our culture, we are under constant bombardment from the media and entertainment industries. These means of communication encourage you to keep those desires and attitudes of the flesh alive. If you continue to indulge those desires, your flesh and those desires will grow. Your appetite for the world will grow each time the desire is fed. If this process continues your flesh will become a raging beast. Its appetite will be insatiable. It will crave more and more until it reaches a nearly unquenchable level. It doesn't happen overnight, but grows in proportion to the amount that it is fed and nurtured. Meanwhile, your spirit man will be reduced to a ninety pound weakling, in intensive care and on life support.

My youngest son, Justin, has a growth disorder. As a parent, you often just have a sense when something just isn't right with one of your kids. My wife and I were extremely concerned when his appetite just wasn't what it should be for a young child at two years old. We wrote it off as a phase he was going through. We initially expressed some concern to our pediatrician, but he indicated it was no big deal so we all moved on. As time went on, his appetite did not return and his body literally stopped growing. We put off the issue and made excuses in our mind as to why he was not growing. In fact, there were extenuating circumstances that we just assumed were a factor in the whole situation. Justin was actually a twin at conception. During the pregnancy, we lost the other child at about fourteen to eighteen weeks. My wife, Diane, went into pre-labor distress and was hospitalized for several days when she was just thirty weeks pregnant. With all the medicines involved in the complications, all the issues that surrounded his conception, birth and subsequent growth we simply attributed it all to the fact that he was just born small and likely always will be small.

For two years we ignored our gut and the obvious physical evidence that was right in front of us each and every day. It wasn't until he was four that we went to see a specialist. That doctor determined that his pituitary gland was functioning at less than ten percent of the capacity it should.

As I mentioned, the obvious physical evidence that my son was not growing was right there in front of our face every day. It was easy to see that our son was small and was not growing. Here is what I want you to understand though; although it was physically obvious that our son was smaller than other kids his age, we had grown accustomed to that fact. It wasn't as obvious anymore, it was expected. It wasn't out of the ordinary, it became ordinary. The same is true as sin, wrong thoughts or attitudes penetrate your being. The longer they exist, the less obvious they become. They become our self-proclaimed "that's just who I am" or are excused as just a part of our personality. That really is the point about being deceived though, because it is the victim that is usually the last one to be aware of it. That is why we *have* to allow the Holy Spirit to provide the input required to awaken us to the deception and excuses that want to invade our spiritual life and take up permanent residence there.

Since we were with our son everyday, it seemed to grow less and less obvious that he wasn't growing. In fact, he had only grown one to two inches over the previous two years. The specialist told us that although he was now four and a half years old, he was only the size of a typical two year old child.

Can you imagine the guilt that my wife and I felt over not getting this checked out earlier? We could tell there were problems, but we made excuses for them. We reasoned with ourselves and convinced ourselves that everything was going to be okay. That is the same kind of attitude that is often taken when it comes to spiritual growth. You know you are not growing spiritually as you should, but you make excuses as to why. Excuses like:

- I'm too busy to go to church
- I just don't have time to read my Bible and spend time with God
- I just can't seem to control my anger
- My thought life leaves a lot to be desired, but is it really hurting anyone?

We could go on and on with examples of the excuses we make for not moving forward and growing as we should. Meanwhile, Jesus is patiently knocking at the door of our heart. Not trying to kick the door in or huffing and puffing to blow it down. He is there, despite our business, despite our distractions, despite our religiosity. I like to say it in these simple terms, God is a gentleman and he will not force Himself on us. He could choose to make us obey His every word. He could strike our hearts with fear. But, the one things God has never chosen to do and never will choose to do, is to make someone love Him.

Instead of making excuses, why not take positive steps forward and resolve the issue? I'll give you the answer that none of us want to hear or admit; because that's the hard way. It would require sacrifice and effort on your part! Not many want to put in the time and effort that is often involved in doing the hard stuff.

Let me get back to the story of Justin. He is now ten years old and he gives himself a growth hormone shot every evening before bedtime. We are extremely pleased to see him growing normally. In fact, he's not only made up for the two years when he barely grew at all, he's surpassed it. He is currently taller than his older brother, Jacob, which doesn't make Jacob happy at all! Within weeks of starting the shot, we noticed he began to have an almost insatiable appetite! He could not go more than one or two hours without nearly coming to tears while describing his hunger. He could nearly eat us out of house and home! With his growth comes a natural hunger to feed the body that is working overtime to grow as it should. It's amazing to me how simple physical principles have parallel principles in the spiritual world. Your spiritual desires act in much the same way. If you feed them, there will rise up a natural almost insatiable appetite for more fuel. The same holds true if you decide to feed those appetites that are opposed to your spiritual growth. Your flesh rarely desires something that will benefit you spiritually. So it goes without saying that growth of your flesh comes at the expense of your spirit. As it grows, it requires more and more attention, more of your time and devotion. All the while, less of your attention, time and devotion will be given to your spiritual growth. Conversely, since the flesh and the spirit are contrary one to another, attention and nurturing that is focused on your spiritual growth is at the expense of growth to the flesh.

None of this should really come as a surprise. What you feed grows and what you ignore withers. How can you maintain the proper focus? There are several ways. First, you must open your eyes to what is going on around you. Secondly, you must be open to the Holy Spirit, always taking an honest look at where you are spiritually. Third, you should find someone to help keep you accountable, a prayer partner or close friend, someone in which you can confide about your struggles. Fourthly, you must fast often.

Fasting is, by today's standards, a lost spiritual discipline. Many refuse to inconvenience themselves with what they consider to be an old fashioned principle. Jesus sure thought it was important enough to practice it himself. Sure, food is a necessity of life, but there is more to life than food and clothing. Jesus set the stage for all His followers, both then and in the future, in Matthew 16:6 (NIV) with an expectation that they should fast. This verse, several others as well, do not beat around the bush, implying it is a good idea or something you may want to try. There is an implication of expectation in the words of Jesus as He begins His statement with, "when you fast." There are some things in life that will require you be willing to fast in order to get the answer, direction or breakthrough you need.

Fasting is designed to *starve* the flesh. It is not a way to lose weight or a means of proving your spiritual superiority to others. In its simplest form, fasting is the willful withholding of food from your body. In practice, you should replace the time you would normally spend eating food for your body with actually feeding your spirit. This can come in various forms: serving, prayer, worship, studying God's word and any variety of other means that would feed your spirit. By replacing the act of *feeding* the flesh with that of *feeding* the spirit you are indeed causing your spirit to grow.

I must add that while fasting has become a lost spiritual discipline, dieting is all the rage these days. Unlike fasting, the fad these days is dieting. There's a diet for everything. There's a diet if you love peanut butter and there is one if you hate it. There is a diet that allows you to eat whatever you want and a diet where no exercise is required. Too many Christians are willing to abstain from eating to try and look better physically, but refuse to fast in order to be better spiritually!

One of the more popular diets is the Atkins diet or some variation of it. The general idea of the diet is to nearly cut carbohydrates out of your diet and concentrate on eating tons of protein. Carbohydrates are basically quick energy for your body. The problem is that most of us do not need quick energy. Quite the opposite, most of us have plenty of fat available to be converted to energy. Protein on the other hand, is fat fighting fuel for your body. I must admit, I have tried this diet. I made it a little over one week once. The first few days weren't too bad, but the more you starve your body from those delicious, mouth-watering carbohydrates, the more your body seems to crave them. I had a natural craving and desire for sweets of all kinds. It can get really bad, so bad that your dreams begin to revolve around Twinkies and Pepsi. All of these same concepts and principles are true when you deny your flesh and move forward in your Christian life. After about two weeks of almost zero carbohydrates in your diet, your body adjusts to the new behavior. The desires never completely go away, but they should become easier to control and manage as you bring them under submission of your choice to abstain.

There will be difficult times and the cravings will actually seem to intensify when things get tough. Take Jesus' experience in the dessert for instance. It's no coincidence that after He had fasted for forty days that Satan first tempted Him with food. Satan isn't stupid! Although not omniscient, he is well aware of areas where you may be weak or where you may tend to struggle. The temptation he brings our way will look appealing. Just like food though, not everything that looks or even tastes good is necessarily good for you.

The process of becoming like Christ is a lifelong mission. Just like with any other venture or experience in life, when you first start out, you can't expect to know it all. Would you be willing to get on a plane if you knew the pilot had flying experience with simulation software on video games but had actually never flown a plane? I hope not. You would trust that any airline pilot trusted to pilot a commercial flight would have extensive training, thousands of hours in the air, not only flying, but assisting and learning from others. Why would you think you know all that you would ever need to know upon your salvation? You will need to learn, grow and experience the pains of life and growth in your Christian walk. Paul wrote to the Christians at Philippi:

> "Dearest friends, you were always so careful to follow my instructions when I was with you. And now that I am away you must be even more careful to put into action God's saving work in your lives, obeying God with deep reverence and fear. For God is working in you, giving you the desire to obey him and the power to do what pleases him"

> (Philippians 2:12–13, nlt)

This process of continual growth and progression in your Christian life is described completely with one big theological term: sanctification. It is the idea of carrying on to perfection the work that began with salvation. This work has a definite beginning in the miracle of salvation and a definite ending in the form of death. All the in between stuff is what you have to work on! The more holy you become by the grace of God, the more humble, self-renouncing, and more sensitive to every sin you become. This will cause you to cling more closely to Christ. Those imperfections that desire to cling to you become more and more annoying as you cry out to Christ for strength to overcome them. It is the loving hand of God, by the Holy Spirit, that brings conviction. It is not, however, designed to bring condemnation, but rather to correct imperfections and confirm God's grace at work in you. It is when you no longer sense the conviction of the Holy Spirit in your life that you really need to be concerned. At that point, you need to take a good, hard, honest look at your life, inviting the Holy Spirit to speak into your life and point out areas needing work or that must change.

Salvation for sinners and sanctification for Christians are mysterious and miraculous works of God. As miraculous as they are, they are just as simply steps in God's plan for man. Although success is promised, it is dependent on two key factors; first, God doing His work in you through the Holy Spirit. Secondly, you must fulfill your responsibility through obedience and discipline.

There is one thing you can be sure of, that God will do His part, but you must be accountable to do your part as well. In your natural way of thinking, there is no desire, hungering or thirsting after His righteousness. It's during the sanctification process that the Holy Spirit puts that hunger, inclination and desire in you. Colossians 3:10 says our mind is being renewed in the "image of its Creator." Your mind is renewed to be like that of Christ. He supplies the grace and strength without which you can do nothing, but with which you can do all things. You just need to open up your eyes to what is available for you and grab hold of it! You need to discipline yourself to continue in the ways of God and set aside those things that interfere.

GET GOING

It's really easy at times to watch from the outside and make judgments or comments about what everyone else is doing. It seems so clear from that perspective as to what the real problems are. It's kind of like that little experience we all had at the age of about sixteen. You know, when you first started driving and your mom (or maybe it was your dad) would bark directions from the passenger seat. Or worse yet, she was in the back seat, leaning up and into your space telling you what to do, where to look and how fast or slow to go! We have probably all had someone in our life that has been a back-seat-driver to us. Mom and dad were on edge during those early driving days and nothing would irritate me more than hearing them bark out instructions about what I was supposed to do. Remember how annoying and frustrating it was? If you choose to look at life from a similar perspective, you could see how at times your reaction to others might be thought of as back-seat-living!

MONDAY MORNING QUARTERBACK

I am a huge sports fan. My family grew up not only revering Sundays as the Sabbath and attending church regularly, but also revering the Sunday NFL countdown! It was all about getting home and sitting in front of the television for the rest of the day. Of course, I wasn't as bad as some, I did usually make it to church for Sunday evening services. Over the years, my love for football has waned and most of my sports affections have turned to hockey. It may seem strange that a guy from Florida would like hockey, but we do have a Stanley Cup title right here in the sunshine state! I mention all that simply to illustrate the art of back-seat-living. Many in the sports world have come to call it the Monday-morning-quarterback syndrome. It involves all those fans that knew exactly why their team lost this past week-end and can't believe their coach is so dumb. There are plenty of fans that call the sports talk radio show that really feel they could have done a better job of coaching the team and are certain they would not have made the same mistake the coach did.

I am guilty of doing this. I see things that seem obvious and wonder why everyone else is so blind they can't see it too. What we need to be careful of is not to just direct everyone else toward change while we remain comfortably in our easy chair, observing from the sideline. Just once, I think it would be funny for a coach, when asked why they made, or didn't make, a certain decision to offer up his job to the person asking the question. I would imagine their debut in the coaching world would likely be a disaster. You can bet it will likely never happen, but I think it would prove to be a memorable experience. It's easy to look in from the outside and make judgments or criticize others for the decisions being made. However, the rules seem to change when it is you that is actually in the game.

I know first hand that it takes a lot more than just being willing to talk about doing something. It takes being willing to get going, step out and put things into motion. As the old adage goes, actions do indeed speak louder than words. If your spouse always told you they loved you but never did anything to show their love for you, would you believe them? Why do we expect

God to believe we love Him when we won't do what He has asked of us? It was Jesus that said in the gospel of John that "if you love me, show it by doing what I've told you". Talk is cheap, just look at the Pharisees. They loved to talk the talk, but all too often (as Jesus constantly pointed out) failed to walk the walk. We expect God to come to our rescue while we burn the hours of our life trying to perform our way into His good graces. That is the place we find our self when we have failed to develop the kind of intimate relationship He desires to have with us. Instead, we have replaced it with a cordial, yet respectful relationship with Him. God isn't excited when you show up at church. He's not even real excited when you drop some money in the offering plate as it comes by. He wants the same intimacy with you that He had with Adam in the Garden of Eden. Somewhere along the way, we became a stranger to God's love and desires, and that soon became a religious pursuit to please God instead of a personal pursuit to connect with Him.

LEFTOVERS

Abraham Lincoln once said good things come to those that wait, but only the things left behind by those that were there before them. I love that quote. It kind of grabs you by surprise. It reminds me of what I like to call spiritual leftovers. There is certainly nothing wrong with leftovers. I'm actually the only one in my family that likes leftovers. They are an automatic, pre-fabricated lunch for the next day. I'm the type of person that will put something leftover in a container and throw it in the refrigerator. A few days later, I'll find it and heat it up. Diane, my wife, on the other hand, will throw anything that has been in the refrigerator for more than twenty-four hours away. She understands better than I do that leftovers are only good for a certain period of time. Once packaged and refrigerated, the natural process of contamination begins to set in. It's not long before the food is no longer any good.

Spiritually speaking, so many Christians have become content with simply going to church and having a good experience. There are many great churches in America. At most of them, you could show up any given week and you would be made to feel good while you are there. Many stop at the experiential level and are simply content with those feelings. There are others that are not there just to feel good, but actually are in pursuit of a real connection with God. Others still sit off on the sideline, content to hang out, observe and feed off the experiences and efforts of others. In a sense, those that become content as observers instead of pursuing their own relationship with God, begin to feed their spirit man with leftovers. They wonder why there is no sense of freshness in their relationship with God. They wonder why even the slightest trial seems to run them off course. They have become content with receiving emotionally from their surroundings and from the experiences of others instead of receiving personally and directly from God through their own personal relationship with Jesus.

Leftovers are a lot easier to prepare than a fresh meal. There isn't a lot of preparation needed to just throw them in the microwave and press a few buttons. The microwave represents a superficial relationship with Jesus. They want to eat, they want to participate, but they don't want to actually work at developing a more intimate relationship with Him. They would rather just warm up to Him on a quick occasion, usually when they need something or have done something wrong. If you are married, you know this statement is true: "Loving, genuine relationships require work!"

James, my favorite New Testament author, proclaimed that faith without works is dead. You can say it as much as you want, but until your lifestyle bears witness to the words from your mouth, your testimony will remain weak at best. When we were youth pastors, Diane and I would take a group of teen-agers to camp each summer. The first year we went, we really didn't know what to expect. We were not disappointed. The Spirit of God moved while we were there. In fact, my wife and I both wondered if maybe we had been more blessed and ministered to than any of the teen-agers we took. We looked forward to camp each and every summer because we knew there would be an opportunity to experience God in a very personal way.

A strange thing happened just shortly before what ended up being our last trip to that summer camp. I was talking with Diane about the whole camp thing and making preparations with her. To my surprise, she told me how much she now hated camp. I was literally in shock by her statement. Of course, I had to know why she had come to this conclusion so I asked her to explain. As she started to explain, her words were very pointed, but very true. Each year we saw teen-ages miraculously saved. Each year we saw teen-ages delivered from a variety of sinful lifestyles and habits. Each year we would see kids getting connected with God. Hundreds of kids were called into the ministry or ministered to in a very special and personal way. Unfortunately, and usually without fail, each year we also witnessed most of the same teen-agers gradually return to their previous lifestyle. While at camp they were constantly in a spiritually charged atmosphere. When they came home and suddenly all the other alternatives were available, they easily crumbled under the pressure to return to their old ways. They just settled back and decided to get reacquainted with their old way of life. They experienced what equated to a spiritual microwave. They rode the emotional timer and then, rather than working at cultivating a lasting, loving relationship with their creator, they just decided it was too hard.

Why do I hate the concept of camp? There are many reasons; I hate hearing how much God has done in lives only to see it wasted and forgotten. I hate hearing people talk about how their lives were changed only for them to slip back into their selfish ways and slap God in the face. I hate that people who know what is right choose not to do it. I hate the unfulfilled potential, the lack of discipline and the relative ease with which many seem to give up on their relationship with God.

This earth is full of many types of natural resources. Forestry, water, precious stones and metals, coal, oil, the list could go on and on. Many of there resources are wasted and taken for granted. I am of the opinion, however, that none of those things represent the greatest natural resource on our earth. The greatest natural resource on our planet is people. The greatest waste of natural resources is the number of people who never achieve their potential in their relationship with God. Complacency can be defined in this simple phrase; choosing to be average. Anyone and everyone can be average, because it doesn't require a whole lot of effort. You could say that average is free, but greatness will cost you something. God has called no one to be average.

TOUGH CHOICES

Society in general today is selfish and self-serving. This is the antithesis of the Christian life, which should be consumed by humility and service to others. I read a story about a young man named Benjamin Landart who, in 1888, was fifteen years old and an accomplished violinist. The story went something like this...

Benjamin lived on a farm in northern Utah with his mother and seven brothers and sisters. This was sometimes a challenge to Benjamin, because he didn't have as much time as he liked to play his violin. Occasionally, his mother would actually lock up the violin until he had his farm chores done, knowing that the temptation for Benjamin to play it was so great.

In late 1892, Benjamin got a chance to travel to Salt Lake to audition for a seat in a local orchestra. For him, this was a dream come true. After several weeks of practicing and prayers, he traveled to Salt Lake in March of 1893 for the much anticipated audition. When he heard Benjamin play, the conductor told Benjamin he was the most accomplished violinist he had heard west of Denver. He was asked to report to Denver for rehearsals in the fall. He would be earning enough money to take care of his needs and have some left over to send home.

A week after Benjamin received the good news, his pastor called him into his office. He had a proposition for Benjamin. He asked if he could put off playing with the orchestra for a couple of years and accept a call to the mission field.

Benjamin felt that giving up his chance to play in the orchestra would be more than he could bear, but he also knew what his decision should be. He promised that if there were any way to raise the money for him to go, he would accept the call.

When Benjamin told his mother about this encounter she was overjoyed. She told him that his father had always wanted to serve as a missionary but had been killed before that opportunity had come to him. Benjamin told her he would not allow her to sell any land in order to raise the money. As she studied his face for a moment, she suddenly had an idea. This family had only one thing that was of great enough value to send Benjamin, his violin.

Ten days later, on March 23, 1893, Benjamin wrote these words in his journal:

"I awoke this morning and took my violin from its case. All day long I played the music I love. In the evening when the light grew dim and I could see to play no longer, I placed the instrument in its case. It will be enough. Tomorrow I leave."

Forty-five years later, on June 23, 1938, Benjamin wrote this in his journal:

> *"The greatest decision I ever made in my life was to give up something I dearly loved to the God I loved even more. He has never forgotten me for it."* 2

Be willing to pay the price. Remember that nothing of value in life will come easily. If you want to accomplish great things, you have to be willing to sacrifice much. The two go hand in hand.

I can say from experience that it would be easy to give up when things don't go your way. Why is it we always just want to quit at the first sign of resistance? If we look at the lives of many of the Old Testament characters, we would see countless cases of men and women rising above the disappointments of life to achieve great and mighty things all for the glory of God. Look at the life of Caleb. It was definitely no cake-walk. Caleb spent the first forty years of his life as a slave amongst the Egyptians. As a forty year old man, Moses sent him out as one of the spies into the Promised Land. Caleb took a stand. Caleb made an unpopular choice to keep going forward. For making the right choice, and doing the right thing, Caleb was rewarded with the privilege of wandering around the dessert for the next forty years. He had forty years to contemplate the decision he made. Just think about the kind of things that would naturally be tossed about in his head. Consider what he may have been thinking; Why should you have to suffer for others disbelief? Maybe you don't really trust God like you should. You must have done something wrong to be treated this way.

How often have you found yourself doubting God because of your circumstances rather than pressing forward? Nothing you go through should intimidate you from standing with your convictions. No amount of frustration should diminish your faith in

God. Caleb chose not to question God or compromise his life in order to make things easier on himself. It seems as though he knew that anything you choose to compromise in order to gain something in life, you will eventually lose.

IN THE BEGINNING

The end of the vision is not the end of this book. Over the last several years, as I have often sat and contemplated what I saw, I have been amazed at how often certain life experiences would draw my attention back to those images I have described. For a long time, I just jotted those things down and threw them in a folder. It wasn't too long ago that I decided to read some of those pages. I knew in my heart that some of those things were things I wanted and needed to communicate to others. Since that decision, God has continued to prompt me with things. I've been awakened in the night with thoughts and ideas. I've been sitting in church and things would flash across my minds eye. I knew I had better write it down or it would soon be forgotten.

Up to this point, everything we have discussed has been simple and to the point. That's not going to change. I am amazed at how often I make easy things difficult! Christianity can be boiled down to some very basic things. But, it is the most basic things that a lot of people seem to struggle with. I know so many intelligent people that lack basic, common sense about life situations. In fact, my wife has accused me (rightfully so at times) of being in that category!

When we make wrong choices or bad decisions, we always seem to try and make up for it by doing stuff. It's similar to the guilty feeling we have when we get into an argument with our spouse or have disappointed them in some way. Our guilt often drives us to do something (or buy something) for them. We think we can somehow get back into their good graces by buttering them up with a gift or act of kindness. It may or may not work with your spouse, but I can assure you, it doesn't work for God. We could never do anything for God that would bring us into His good graces. It is His extension of divine mercy and grace, as well as the sacrificial offering of His one and only Son, Jesus, that enables us to be called the children of God.

Keith Green wrote a song years ago that I love. It was titled: "To obey is better than sacrifice." My favorite line in that song says this: *"He doesn't need your money… He wants your life…"*

With God, it's so much less about what or how much you do and so much more about who you really are. All the money in the world when you are dead will do you no good. Sure, it will help take care of your family, buy you a nice headstone and a catchy epitaph. But, it has no eternal value. A good name and godly character is a lifelong heritage to be admired by generations.

Who you are is determined by your character. Your character is determined by your choices. Your choices are ultimately determined by your faith. If who you are does not line up with what you say or how you live, it will eventually catch up to you. You must always choose obedience to God over sacrifice for God. Let me say it again so it sinks in… you must always choose obedience *to* God over sacrifice *for* God.

Too many Christians are concerned about what they are missing out on in this world instead of what they are missing out on with God. They consider the fact they are a Christian as a sacrifice in and of itself. They consider a few hours at church per week a sacrifice. They consider reading God's Word instead of watching television a sacrifice. All of these things are indeed a sacrifice when viewed through the perspective of someone that feels obligated to God. This is the perspective of someone that has become a stranger to the things of God. Intimacy with God is not different than intimacy with a person. The most important thing there is to developing an intimate relationship is time— Unrushed, unstructured, uninterrupted time. Too many of us allow life's circumstances to get us so busy that we substitute spending time with God our self everyday with just going to church. We replace personal worship and religious rituals. All of a sudden, our intimate relationship takes on a business casual flair. We stop telling God how we really feel and start telling God what we think He wants to hear.

Start to understand the privilege it is to love and be loved by God. Begin to contemplate the depth of God's grace, mercy and forgiveness. Instead of being worried about what we are missing out on out there, let's start being consumed with submitting our life, every part of it, to God.

THE DEPARTURE

I want to take some time to go back to the beginning. Think back with me to how this whole thing started. Even from the very beginning of time it seems that mankind has struggled with obedience. Simple things become difficult when your perspective is self-serving rather than self-sacrificing.

Just imagine with me for a minute what it would be like if you were able to walk beside and commune with God. The joy and fulfillment that would consume you everyday as God would come and join you for a walk in the cool of the day. You could talk about your day, about things you saw and did, or maybe about your future. There would be times when you would just go for a leisurely stroll with Him to enjoy His company and fellowship. I can't imagine ever getting tired of being in such close and intimate relationship with God. That is exactly the type of intimate relationship Adam and Eve were privileged enough to originally have with God. There was peace and tranquility everywhere on earth, including in the heart of man. Times were good. So good, in fact, they couldn't get any better.

The earth was created with perfection in the mind of God and it was His intention that everything stay that way. In this world as it was created, there was only one simple rule for mankind to follow. Thinking about it in that light, it certainly doesn't seem like it was too much to ask. The rule was very specific and very simple. There was no hidden agenda or room for misinterpretation. Adam and Eve were allowed to eat anything the earth had to offer except for the fruit from one specific tree in the middle of the garden. That tree was called the tree of the knowledge of good and evil. The entire world was at their disposal and only the fruit of one tree was off limits. The possibilities were endless. All the things they could do, the places they could go and the things they could see should have kept them busy for decades without ever having to pass by that one specific tree. It wasn't too long before the smooth talking enemy lured them to the tree. I have a feeling that it was actually a combination of the smooth talking enemy and the natural enticement to something that is forbidden that drew them close to the tree.

If they had only stopped to consider God's one simple rule. Surely they knew that God had never lied to them or disappointed them. There was absolutely no reason not to trust and believe every word He said. So why did they so easily do exactly what God instructed them not to do? In just a few short sentences Eve was convinced that God was not telling them the truth. It wasn't long at all after the miraculous 6 days of creation that mankind sinned and created a natural gap by which sin was introduced into the world. Ever since that point in time, it has been sin that separated mankind and God from having that close and intimate relationship.

At this point, it would be easy to try and point the finger at Eve and blame her for this whole mess. That's too easy, besides the fact that it's not actually accurate. If you read the account in Genesis, the Bible actually indicates that Adam was right there with Eve when all this happened. Evidently, he too was preoccupied and fascinated with what the enemy said. So much so that he did not care for and protect his wife. He allowed himself to be distracted. His distraction allowed to happen what should have never happened. Immediately after he allowed the unthinkable, he actually did the inconceivable. He did what he knew was not right. Adam, as are father's and husband's everywhere, was called to be the priest of his home. Adam should have been the one to confront and denounce the enemy. The devil himself came to deceive Eve, but it was Adam that was not prepared to handle the situation. Both Adam and Eve failed to do what they knew in their heart was right. Instead, they set the example for all of mankind by giving in to the seduction and temptation of this world. As the events that followed progressed, Adam and Eve also progressed in their newly found wrong ways. Not only did they try to hide from God out of guilt and shame, they chose to blame everyone else instead of taking responsibility for their own actions and choices. We certainly have continued to master that pattern of futility well into the 21st century.

Eve's first mistake was in touching the fruit. Satan knew that if he could get Eve to touch the fruit, it was the first step in getting her to eat it. God clearly indicated in Genesis chapter 2 that they were not to eat of the fruit from that tree. It was Eve in Genesis chapter 3, when responding to Satan, who added the emphasis indicating the fruit was not even to be touched. The fruit was no doubt alluring. It was pleasant to look at. The same is true with temptation (as well as sin) in general. The initial temptation will not only be alluring, but downright attractive. It will not come packaged with a skull and cross bones insignia. It will be shiny not dull. It will seem delightful, delicate and dainty, not dirty, dark and dingy.

Such was the picture painted by the serpent and such was the fall of mankind. The simple truth of the matter is that Eve allowed herself to be captivated by the idea that God was some-how not telling her and Adam the truth. The delivery was in a much prettier package than that, but that was simple truth of the matter. She fixed her gaze upon the fruit. Almost immediately, there was birthed inside of her a desire for what that fruit had to offer. That desire grew into lust; that lust begat an illegitimate sense of need. In her mind it was as though, all of a sudden, there seemed to be a void in her life without that fruit. Suddenly, she couldn't live without it. Inevitably, when you fix your gaze on something (and in return, you take it off Jesus), it often creates a sense of desire in you as well. So, you must always be careful to guard your mind, or as Peter says it, "gird up the loins of your mind" (1 Peter 1:13, KJV).

The nation of Israel had a natural inclination toward lazi-ness and the easy ways of life. This type of mindset set them up for many difficult situations. Lot's penchant for success and acceptance caused him to pitch his tent toward Sodom. It was what he focused on, the first thing he saw when he got up in the morning and it was the last thing he saw before he went to bed at night. He set his gaze upon it. Samson's penchant for power and sex caused him to involve himself with numerous women God had forbidden him to involve himself with. His focus led to him breaking his Nazarene vows, which ultimately led to God removing His anointing and power from his life. Unfortunately, Samson did not even notice until it was too late! Judges 16:20 is what I like to call one of the saddest moments in the Bible. Samson assumed he could get himself out of his predicament as he had in the past. He had been there before and was always able to get out of any trouble he found himself in. This time, he did not realize the Spirit of the Lord had left him. He was preoccupied and focused on everything else. He didn't have time to worry about God. So much so, he didn't realize the favor and hand of God had been removed from his life.

These examples do serve a purpose. They remind us that the ways of man are rooted in selfishness. Selfishness is the ultimate form of idolatry. It elevates you to a position above God. This is why Satan himself was removed from heaven. It is pride and selfishness that often stands in the way of someone coming to know Jesus. It has become the American way, the battle cry of our humanistic society…"I got myself into this, so I will get myself out." Contrary to the humanistic ways of our day, the Bible says that without Christ, I can do nothing. It further assures us that I can do all things through Him who gives me strength. In a fit of selfishness, it's pride that says "I can do it by myself" or "I know what's best for me."

THE GIRDLE PARABLE

The book of Jeremiah is my favorite Old Testament book. It seems each time I read any part of that book, I learn something new. Once, in an afternoon, I sat down and read the whole book in one sitting. It was during that reading that I began to notice a pattern of straying by the Israelites. In chapters 2–11 specifically, I noticed the various ways in which Israel strayed from their relationship with God. I also noticed for the first time some very unique things about the tribe of Judah. There was an obvious separation or delineation between themselves and the rest of Israel. This tribe is the ancestral lineage of Jesus. The people of

Judah, that should have been the closest to God, those that were in the direct lineage of Christ, were actually in worse condition than the rest of Israel.

Your Bible may have headings throughout the text designed to describe sections of scriptures. I've developed a pattern over the years of giving sections of scriptures my own personal nicknames. There is one such section in Jeremiah chapter 13 that I have affectionately come to call "the girdle parable." The simplicity of the message of that text is found in verse 11:

> "For as the girdle cleaveth to the loins of a man, so have I caused to cleave unto me the whole house of Israel and the whole house of Judah, saith the LORD; that they might be unto me for a people, and for a name, and for a praise, and for a glory: but they would not hear"

(Jeremiah 13:11, KJV)

I find myself chuckling every time I read it. I get a picture in my mind of trying to squeeze myself into one of those things we call a girdle. The mental pictures I get involve a lot of wiggling, squirming and it's all just a little uncomfortable. Guys just aren't really meant to be wearing those things! There's not a much clearer picture of something being really close to a man than that.

The picture of that vivid image in my mind is the kind of closeness I want to be impressed in your mind as you read these words. . He wants a relationship that is genuine, sincere and wholehearted. He is and always has been calling out to us. Unfortunately, too many of us ignore Him. If you look closely at the scripture from Jeremiah above it finishes with "but they would not hear." The implication in that sentence is that they really could hear Him if they chose to. Their choice was to ignore God's call, His voice, His desire, His Word. Once they were confronted with the truth there was nothing they could really do or say to justify their choices. Just as I was embarrassed when considering myself in a girdle, there is something about a genuine, intimate relationship with God through Jesus Christ that makes the uncommitted feel uncomfortable.

The Israelites, especially the tribe of Judah, knew what God wanted and expected from them. They knew better than to make wrong choices and decisions. Even though they knew all this, they did it anyway. Too many people that consider themselves Christians live their life at that same level in their relationship with God. They know what God's Word says, but because they remain committed to their relationship with Him at somewhere less than one-hundred percent, closeness to God makes them uncomfortable. Being in God's presence gives them an uneasy feeling. They retain a superficial relationship with Him simply because they realize they need one. Because of their understanding, they also know they are not where they need to be in their relationship with Him. It happens to Christians all around America. They justify it in their own mind, but once you actually write it out on paper, it really doesn't make any sense.

After really aching over this problem, I have come to know there are four types of people that call themselves Christians.

The first is the "No-weather Christian". These people claim to be Christians because they believe it is one of their inalienable rights that are due to them as an American citizen. They don't go to church but consider themselves a good person. They've never done anything they really consider to be extremely sinful. Extreme sins to them would be something like murder. They have no problem with telling little white-lies, cheating on their taxes or fantasizing about their neighbor's spouse. After all, they justify to themselves that those types of things don't really hurt anyone! It is the epitome of the worldly way of thinking today: Let me do what I can get away with, not what is right, because, after all, what is right is actually subjective and relative to your own personal opinion. Situational ethics and loose morality mark the norm with type of person.

The second type is the "Fair-weather Christian". This person has no problem serving and living for God when things are going well and the weather is good. As soon as the storm clouds roll in and the clasps of thunder can be heard, they whine, complain and tend to blame God for their circumstances. This person is always in church; in fact they may serve in many capacities at their church. The problem lies in their heart. This type of person is never content and often grumbles or complains when things are not going their way. They see people as a means to get their way. Unfortunately, they see God in pretty much the same light. The danger with this type of person is that they are often convinced their religiosity and superficial duties equate to salvation. This type of person may have often grown up in the church. Their familiarity with church life causes them to live religiously but never really have a life changing encounter with God. Because of the lack of a real relationship with Jesus, they do not live in the power of the Spirit, but on their own power. This causes frustration when things don't go their way and they can't fix their own problems, so they blame God. They live in the disappointing and delusional lifestyle of self-fulfillment.

The third type is the "Foul-weather Christian". This person is the opposite of the "Fair-weather Christian". They are content to do as they please while things are good and the weather is clear. This time, when the storm clouds roll in and the clasps of thunder begin to be heard, they find themselves at the altar begging God to be involved in their life. It's almost like they treat God like a genie in a bottle and when they need something, they start rubbing. As soon as the weather clears and their problems seem to be over, they are back to living life as they please. I've seen this kind of response countless times. I've seen people who have lost their job, show up in church, visit the altar, get a new job and never set another foot inside the church… until the next dilemma hits! I've seen it happen when marriages are in danger of divorce, when someone has gotten into legal trouble, I could go on and on with the examples. This person only partially understands their need for a relationship with God through Jesus Christ. They see no reason to serve God when things are well. Prayer and a relationship with Jesus is not a magical formula to get what you want. Using God in crisis mode is a dangerous way to live. It is God's intention that He be your sustenance and source of strength, direction and inspiration on a daily basis, not just when the going gets tough.

Last, is the "All-weather Christian." This is someone that understands their need for God. Paul described this type of attitude when he wrote to the church at Philippi, he said:

> "Not that I was ever in need, for I have learned how to get along happily whether I have much or little. I know how to live on almost nothing or with everything. I have learned the secret of living in every situation, whether it is with a full stomach or empty, with plenty or little. For I can do everything with the help of Christ who gives me the strength I need"

> (Philippians 4:11–13, NLT)

These people are my heroes! They have come to the place in their life where nothing matters as much to them as pleasing God. They have turned their back on the religiosity that comes from a superficial relationship with Him. They have replaced that with the contentment of the knowledge that as a child of God, His hand is intimately involved in each and every aspect of their life. No matter what weather comes their way, they are equipped like all-terrain vehicles, ready for any type of conditions. They press on, carrying out their everyday lives regardless of the weather.

It's all a matter of perspective. Some don't want God interfering with their life. Some just want God to be there when they need Him. It all boils down to a relationship with Jesus Christ that is measured not by how much you have of Him, but by how much of you He has.

SUPERMEN

Many Christians today have somehow come to the conclusion that they can not rise above the worldly culture and influence of this day. They somehow doom themselves to failure. They just assume they are going to fail and that distance in their relationship with God is a foregone conclusion. Let me say clearly that we aren't expected to be perfect! That should be a refreshing revelation. God never expects us to be perfect, but we are expected to be on a path in pursuit of perfection. We can't be supermen, but then again, God never really expected us to be in the first place. Those kinds of expectations are self-imposed.

There is not an excuse under the sun that has not been used before. I don't think anyone could come up with an excuse that God's Word doesn't cover in some form or fashion. Has God changed since the beginning of time? I don't think so. Has He suddenly stopped working in people's lives? I don't think so. W. Phillip Keller said:

> "We live in a day, when as of old, God is looking for men and women of fearless faith, who will step out to achieve

great things for Him. God has not changed since the time of Joshua, nor does He honor faith less now than He did then. It is simply a case of coming to a place where we will walk with Christ by faith rather than by sight."[3]

Why are we any different than the great men and women of the Old Testament? For that matter, why are we any different from the disciples and others in the New Testament after the day of Pentecost? The power that Jesus instructed them to wait for, the power of the infilling of the Holy Spirit that fell on them that day, is still available today. It is the power that will enable you to be a witness and live a blameless life in pursuit of God. When you look at the lives of the disciples, their lives are only moving in one direction after this unique experience. We see the mighty power of God at work in and through them. We see men and women, just like you and me, willing to die for the cause of Christ. Where has that kind of passion for the lost gone? Where has that degree of desire to please God at any cost gone? It is largely absent from Christians in America and the American church as a whole. Unfortunately, consistency in the things that will bring us closer to Him, things like faith, obedience, the pursuit of holiness, have become the exception for many rather than normal behavior.

THE WARNING

Once the departure from God's plan was initiated, things had to change. No longer would mankind be allowed the intimacy with God that was His original design. No longer could man stay in the Garden of Eden. No longer would the earth provide for man. Mankind was cursed to work and toil in order to receive the fruit of the earth. Man would be charged with a life sentence of hard labor, eating only by the sweat of his brow. The years of his life would be numbered at the end of which, he would return to the dust from which he was created.

HEAR YE, HEAR YE

A new type of relationship with God had to be developed. Things would never be the same. Mankind would never be able to communicate with God as Adam and Eve did in the Garden. This departure from God's plan called for a mediator, or someone to stand in the gap between God and man. Throughout the Old Testament, God used a mediator, even to communicate with His people. This mediator was at times a leader, like Moses. Other times it was a Judge, like Ruth. Still other times it was a prophet, like Elijah. In addition to using a mediator for communication, God also chose to use the tabernacle and the most holy place as a mediator for His presence. Certain individuals were appointed as priests and tended to the things of God. The single-threaded nature of this type of communication and habitation served its purpose for a time. Then came the time and need for change. Jesus Christ was sent to become the New Covenant, the New Testament, the one mediator between God and man. The writer of Hebrews said:

> "So Christ has now become the High Priest over all the good things that have come. He has entered that great, perfect sanctuary in heaven, not made by human hands and not part of this created world. Once for all time he took blood into that Most Holy Place, but not the blood of goats and calves. He took his own blood, and with it he secured our salvation forever. Under the old system, the blood of goats and bulls and the ashes of a young cow could cleanse people's bodies from ritual defilement. Just think how much more the blood of Christ will purify our hearts from deeds that lead to death so that we can worship the living God. For by the power of the eternal Spirit, Christ offered himself to God as a perfect sacrifice for our sins"

(Hebrews 9:11–14, NLT)

The problem is the same as it has always been. Man chooses to ignore the means and ways God has established for us to build a relationship with Him. The fact that sin separates mankind from God is ignored. Too many people give no effort at a relationship with Jesus except the occasional half-hearted request for forgiveness or the sudden whole-hearted request for an emergency or an urgent personal need. They fully expect that with the snap of a finger, God will make everything okay. His Word clearly lays out the requirements for forgiveness, restoration and true repentance. "Then if my people who are called by my name will humble themselves and pray and seek my face and turn from their wicked ways, I will hear from heaven and will forgive their sins and heal their land" (2 Chronicles 7:14, NLT).

Yes, the way to forgiveness through repentance was established in the Old Testament. Too many Christians today do not completely understand what unconfessed sin does to their relationship with God. American Christians accept sin as common place and acceptable. It is only when you have come to fully understand how much God detests sin and how much He loves you that you are prepared for true repentance. Instead of expecting God's forgiveness, all of us need to be broken by the fact that we have offended almighty God when we allow sin to remain in our life. Instead of relying on God's infinite mercy, we must also remember that He is just. Sin becomes common place and accepted in the life of those that take His forgiveness for granted. They come to think of sin as a necessary evil and even justify their actions, thoughts and attitudes by assuming there will always be an opportunity to breathe a quick "I'm sorry," making everything okay.

It's a misconception to assume you will be able to invoke a relationship with God through Jesus when you are ready, on your own terms. A lack of disdain for sin points directly to a heart that has come to expect God's forgiveness! It's an attitude that almost says "I'm going to have my fill of fun and then I'll think about getting my life turned around." It was very early in the Bible that God mentioned His Spirit will not always reach out and touch the heart of man. Later in the New Testament, He indicates that no one can come to the Father unless the Spirit draws him. If you read the second half of the first chapter of Romans, it is a very scary section of scripture. It refers to those that know about God, but refuse to honor Him as God. Those that know are accountable, they're held responsible for that knowledge. Those that refuse to handle that knowledge effectively fall into a dangerous category. When you try to put God on your timetable and place him at your beckon call, it is a very dangerous place to live.

Sin interferes with our ability to hear from God. In the twelfth chapter of Romans, it opens by asking us to present our bodies as a living sacrifice to God. Think about those words for a minute and allow them to penetrate your mind. If you take a look at the words individually and consider what they mean, it seems a little ironic. A sacrifice is usually thought of as dead, but Paul specifically indicates that our bodies are to be a *living* sacrifice. In my mind, I picture this as a battle between the spirit and the flesh. The flesh must continually be overcome and suppressed or it is just going to jump off of the altar. Our flesh is that part of us which always seems to lean toward sin and selfishness. Paul didn't stop with verse one though, he continued, "don't copy the behavior and customs of this world, but let God transform you into a new person by changing the way you think. Then you will know what God wants you to do, and you will know how good and pleasing and perfect his will really is" (Romans 12:2, NLT).

This verse simply confirms the idea that we are not to be like everybody else. There must be a visible, obvious difference between those that have a relationship with God through Jesus and those that have not. This is the problem with the Christian in America. Those differences have become blurry. No longer are there clear moral differences between those that call themselves Christian's and those that do not.

Christians that play with sin like a toy are playing a deadly game. Sin will not only interfere with your relationship with God, but causes several other issues. It will alienate you from Godly people. When you have sin in your life, you don't want to be around people that make you feel guilty. It's easier to keep your distance so you feel better about yourself. It's easier to justify your actions to yourself than have to answer to anyone else.

Sin in your life will also diminish your view of God's principles. God's ways, thoughts and commands will no longer hold the importance they once did. The more you act on temptation, the easier it becomes to act on the next time. It's just like riding a bike or driving a car, the more you do it, the better you get at it. The more prevalent it becomes, the more distance you'll find in your relationship with God. That alienation feeds the flesh and creates a diminished capacity to understand God's ways. Look at this verse written to the Christians in Corinth:

> "Dear brothers and sisters, when I was with you I couldn't talk to you as I would to mature Christians. I had to talk as though you belonged to this world or as though you were infants in the Christian life. I had to feed you with milk and not with solid food, because you couldn't handle anything stronger. And you still aren't ready, for you are still controlled by your own sinful desires. You are jealous of one another and quarrel with each other. Doesn't that prove you are controlled by your own desires? You are acting like people who don't belong to the Lord"

> (1 Corinthians 3:1–3, NLT)

Let's go back to Jeremiah for a moment. Chapter fourteen describes a drought that was in the land. Things were so bad that animals were abandoning their young because there wasn't enough food and water. In the midst of all this turmoil, you would think people would begin to sense there are some problems. At least maybe the *Christians* would understand something needs to change, right? Wrong! Just like we do today, instead of seeing the need for change, they want God to bail them out. In fact, we go even one step further; we don't just ask Him to do it, we expect Him to do it! In this text, God was trying to get their attention. He wanted them to understand they didn't need to pray for a blessing or a way out of their situation, they needed to see the error of their ways. God actually told Jeremiah not to pray for them anymore. It's a pretty major thing to consider that God was that serious about this whole situation. He indicated He would ignore their pleas and continue the ways of difficulty in their lives. The people, however, didn't believe Jeremiah when he relayed that information. In fact, the other *prophets* of that day were all telling the Israelites that everything was going to be just fine. At the end of verse 13, they actually say "the LORD will surely send you peace." Here are *prophets,* supposedly dedicated to God and carrying out His service, but they are lying for the sake of comforting the people. They simply told the people exactly what they wanted to hear.

God's intent in warning is always to bring about change and correction. We could go on through Jeremiah and talk about the more warnings to leaders (chapter twenty-three) and more false prophecies (chapter twenty-eight), but the principles are all the same. There is no new way to lie to or deceive God. They have all been tried before in some form or fashion.

You will know that you are serious about changing your life when you stop making excuses for your behavior. The apostle Paul is a perfect example. His trip down the Damascus road led to a divine encounter. Sure, it's not ever day that we're struck with blindness or hear a divine, audible voice speak to us. It is, however, a common experience to feel the conviction of the Holy Spirit regarding issues in our lives. The simple question to ask is; how is that any different than Paul's experience on the way to Damascus? Conviction is God's primary means of warning us. We must heed those warnings. Paul's encounter on that road was a life-changing encounter with Jesus Christ. He was never the same after that journey. His personality, his plans and his life purpose were all changed. Paul not only heard the warning, but listened as well. God pursued Paul and Paul returned the favor. That's exactly how it should be.

TAG, YOU'RE IT

Did you ever play tag as a kid? It seemed that there was an end-less array of spin-offs from that one simple little game. There was hide-and-go-seek, kick the can, freeze tag, capture the flag, got-you-last (on of my family's favorites) and many more. I could devote a chapter to describing the various iterations of what boils down to a pretty simple game conceptually. Tag is a very simple game, with simple rules. If you are the one that is designated as being "it", you are the pursuer. Everyone else in the game will be pursued. As the pursuer, you catch others by tagging them. Immediately the roles reverse—the pursuer is now pursued by the pursued that has become the pursuer (I don't think I could type that again, much less say it!). You get the idea—you try your best not to get touched by the person that is it, only to be in hot pursuit of everyone that is not it when you are. We try to make the idea of God and being a Christian really difficult. In actual-ity, the whole thing is very simple. There aren't a lot of rules to follow, just be in constant pursuit of Him. You're it! The good news is that God, by His very nature, whether He is *it* or not, is always pursuing you! There are many parallels to this game and the ways so many choose to try and live out their Christian life.

THE CHASE

It is often in the midst of despair and difficulty that divine intervention becomes an object of pursuit. Remember the foul-weather Christian? In times such as this, there is nothing that could keep them from pursuing the intervention of God in their circumstances. There is no obstacle they will not try to overcome; there is no length they will not traverse in their pursuit of God. Of course, that needs to be our attitude when there is a need! It is amazing to me, so I can only imagine what God thinks when He is so easily tossed to the side when our sea of circumstances begins to calm down. Despite the relative ease by which mankind can forget his need for a savior, the good news is that He is in constant pursuit of us. It is God's will that none should perish, but all come to repentance. It is in that frame of reference that we can say He is constantly pursuing a deeper and more committed relationship with us.

C.S. Lewis was a very influential and well-known Christian author through the 20th century. The main thrust of his ministry was spiritual growth. Many do not realize that as a teenager, Lewis was actually a professing atheist. Once converted, his theology was very simple—he obeyed God because God was God. After all, if God is God, He must be obeyed—not for the sake of any other reason other than the fact that He is God. As a young man, Lewis insisted he was not seeking God. Instead, it was God that was seeking Him. Once, during the chase, he responded. At that point, he also submitted, and the rest is history.

The very impulse to think about God comes from God Himself. In fact, the desire to discover the truth and understand reality is born from Him. It was Jesus that said, "People can't come to me unless the Father who sent me draws them to me" (John 6:44, NLT). The Lord said through Isaiah, "People who never before inquired about me are now asking about me. I am being found by people who were not looking for me. To them I have said, 'I am here!'" (Isaiah 65:1, NLT). He is always in pursuit of us and will do whatever it takes to get our attention. That does not mean we will respond and make the right choice, only that God will assure the conditions are such that we are always able to make the right decision. We must have the moral courage to actually make that right choice and carry through on it!

THE RIVER

In Ezekiel chapter 47, we find some very descriptive analogies between the presence of God and a river. Actually, this passage is referring back to Ezekiel chapter 40 when he indicated that God gave him a series of visions that he was to communicate to Israel. This is just one of many he went on to describe in this seven chapters that God showed him. Ezekiel went on to describe the water that flowed from the Temple of God in four stages. It all began in water that was ankle deep. Then he was led to a place where the water was knee deep, then to a place up to his waist and finally to a place where the water was over his head.

The application of this passage is simple. There are levels to which we can go and enjoy the presence of God. The further we go, the more we are enveloped with God's presence. Each successive level requires more commitment and more work on our part. Why would any Christian be content to splash around in what amounts to a kiddy pool of God's presence? You know the pool I'm talking about. It's the shallow, easily navigated, warm one. At its deepest point it may reach 6 inches. This is perfect for small children to wade in, sit in and splash around. There is little danger and it requires nearly no commitment to learn any kind of swimming technique. In the kiddy pool, all you did is sit around and splash.

Ezekiel described it as ankle deep. Don't get me wrong, it is certainly in the presence of God, but there is so much more available for those that are willing to move forward in their pursuit of Him. Shallow Christians become content right here in this kiddy pool. They are happy to receive the occasional sprinkle or splash of His presence. They pursue their relationship with Him at this very superficial level. Even though the amount they receive is miniscule, they are content to just be there. They consider themselves to have reached the pinnacle of His presence but are in fact content to dwell in a shallow, occasional relationship with Him. Their pursuit stops as soon as they get a taste or sprinkle of His presence and power. A little bit is good enough for them. God, on the other hand, is always ready to give us more. He is in constant pursuit of us, in hopes that we will return the favor.

When you settle for just a little sprinkling of God's presence in your life, you run the risk of creating huge problems. Living in Florida, we occasionally experience a geographic event called a sinkhole. Florida as a geographic body is near sea level and not very dense. Under the crust of the surface are tunnels and collections of water called aquifers. Water flows through these areas and collects in order to supply the surrounding areas with water. Some of these aquifers are as wide as rivers and flow for miles. During the dry seasons, the aquifers will often subside or dry up all together. When this happens, it leaves a void beneath the surface. If the flow of water does not return to fill the void, the infrastructure ultimately will weaken which will lead to a total collapse. When the collapse occurs, it exposes the vastness of the void beneath the surface. What was invisible one moment suddenly can swallow up roads, trees and houses. It is no different when we look at the river of God's presence in our lives. Without a constant flow of God's presence in our lives, we develop a void. That void can only be filled by the river of His presence. When you settle for a trickle, you run the risk of creating a weak structure that will ultimately collapse.

This chase and pursuit of His presence requires persistence. In Luke 11:9–10, we hear from Jesus' own mouth that we not only *ask*, but we must keep on asking. We must not only *seek*, but we must keep on seeking. We must not only *knock*, but we must keep on knocking, pressing, persisting, still knocking at the same door, and we will, even if it takes great lengths and tremendous efforts and sacrifices, we will prevail. A little further in the gospel of Luke we find Jesus telling the story of the persistent widow. It starts like this, "One day Jesus told his disciples a story to illustrate their need for constant prayer and to show them that they must never give up" (Luke 18:1, NLT).

Prayer is the lifeline in your relationship with God. We are to remain in a constant attitude of prayer throughout the day as well as to connect with Him personally in private, intimate prayer time. It has to be daily, hourly, minute- by- minute. It's our way to communicate with God. As such, it is not something we should grow tired of doing. It is not something we should put off until a crisis comes. It is our responsibility to communicate in such a way as to develop an intimate relationship with God through Jesus Christ. Think of it in terms of a relationship between a father and son. As a teenager, if my son wants to be able to ask for the keys to my car on Friday, he had certainly better be communicating with me Monday through Thursday. If he expects to come home Monday through Thursday without uttering a word and shut himself up in his room every night, he's in for a rude awakening. He can't just kick back and do nothing around the house. He can't take his dinner to his room every night. He can't ignore his mother and I completely on Monday through Thursday and expect us to meet his demands, when he need something on Friday. That is no way to develop a relationship. You will never get to a level of intimacy and trust that is needed acting that way. It doesn't work that way with God either.

Unlike the persistent widow in the parable above, many Christians seem embattled, dejected, depressed and ready to give up. Even on their best days, their relationship with God is stale and lifeless. Instead of moving forward in their relationship, they just stand still as if unprepared to do or say anything. Their lives are just one defeat after another and one bout with despair and depression after another. So many pastors spend countless hours catering to Christians that are indulging in self-pity. Pastors are supposed to be challenging people to move forward in their relationship with God. Because so many lack emotional maturity, pastors are required to constantly cater to their needs. It's the "quick fix" mindset that permeates the American Christians today. They want to spout off all their problems and then leave their session with a magic pill to solve everything. After all, the world already spends billions of dollars on physical impotence; why not try to find a magic pill for spiritual impotence too? Thank goodness He does not give up on us, but rather is patient with us, calling us away form despair and defeat, into the victory He has already secured on our behalf.

Pursuing God is sometimes the most difficult when things are going fairly well. It is human nature to kind of relax when things are going good. We tend to let our guard down. Persistence comes a little easier when times are tough. After all, that is when you really do need someone to help. It's the times when things are good that even the best of men can grow lackadaisical in their love for and pursuit of God. It's during those moments of ease that we can learn who we really are.

Phillip Keller said: "Very often amid affluence, ease and relative peace, human beings tend to settle down softly and take their heritage very much for granted. What men lay down their lives for in battle is sometimes obscured and overlooked amid our affluence. Often truth itself is lost more readily in the lap of luxury than it ever is in the clash of battle. God's word does not change whether our lives are in danger or in security."[4]

Too many are off seeking signs and wonders, blessings and miracles, but aren't willing to put forth enough effort in maintaining their day to day relationship with God. They will cry out to God when it is convenient for them or when they need something; otherwise they remain in what amounts to a spiritual comma.

It is all too easy to be corrupted by complacency because all it requires you to do is absolutely nothing! God's ultimate purpose is not that we simply make it through life, but that we live an overcoming life that is set free from the influences of the world. He wants us to find fulfillment, rest and fruitful lives rich in the abundance of His provision. He is constantly stirring us to seek higher ground, to enter into the rich, abundant life He offers and to find contentment in Him.

This type of contentment is, simply speaking, spiritual contentment. It is developed deep within the soul of those whose quiet confidence rests completely in God. It has nothing to do with happiness. The very idea that happiness is synonymous with contentment is ludicrous. Happiness depends upon what is happening around you. It is rooted in and reflective of your situation, circumstances and earthly relationships. Joy and contentment are based on your relationship with God. It is rooted in the fact that He is ultimately in control and your life is in His hands. Many Christians do not develop their relationship with Him enough to ever experience true joy and contentment. Too many have never learned to fully trust Him for victory in the middle of life's conflicts. They have not come to the place where they can obey His wishes no matter the situation they find themselves in. They still try to resolve their problems with their own human resources, rather than trusting in someone they can not see. They stop pursuing God in their everyday life and are content with a casual, Sunday morning only relationship with Him.

My family and I are currently in ministry transition. There have been some very difficult times. We sold our house and moved from a very comfortable place, for no reason other than that was what God was speaking to our hearts. We are currently renting a house that is right on a golf course. That may sound like a great place for a lot of pastors, but I have never picked up a golf club in my life! The house is across a small lake just after a dogleg bend along the 13th fairway. This setting, on the golf course by a lake, has been extremely gratifying to me. I've always been a nature lover. I think I got that from my grandmother on my dad's side. Grammy, as we called her while growing up, would spend hours early in the mornings walking the beach of Fenwick Island Delaware. She would collect whatever trinkets the sea had washed up on the shore from the night before (I still have a few of those trinkets from her adventures to this day). Besides her long walks on the ocean shore, she and my grandfather were very avid bird watchers. They would intently watch a variety of species pick through the food items they would leave on the railing of the balcony. Grammy always seemed to have time to observe nature. It is something I have learned to enjoy as well—just observing the beauty of God's creation.

In our current living situation, I often find myself on the back patio just sitting, relaxing and observing. I watch and hear frustrated golfers as their white dimpled balls plop into the water, hit a nearby neighbor's roof or end up in one of the many sand traps. In order to truly relax and enjoy myself, I have to tune all of that out. Once I am "in the zone" I can watch the alligator patrol the shores of the lake or a variety of bird species interact with one another and carry on their daily routines. There is one specific species of bird that I have really grown to appreciate, the purple martin. That appreciation began as a young boy growing up in Martinsburg, West Virginia. My grandfather and my father both used special birdhouses to attract the purple martins to nest and settle in their area. In saying all of this, I'm not trying to identify some type of whimsical obsession with a bird that actually appears to be mostly black in color, not purple! There are reasons to desire these birds to make their homes near yours. The purple martins diet consists entirely of flying insects. They are notoriously hungry birds and they eat what most people consider to be notoriously pesky insects. Besides their pleasant diet, they also produce a very pleasant song.

All this talk of nature sure is making it hard for me to concentrate. In a great display of learned behavior, I too have a bird house specifically designed to attract purple martins! Just after we moved in to this rental house, I put the bird house up in the back yard out by the lake. Just about four weeks ago, I heard the familiar song of the purple martin while I was out in the yard one day. Since then, we have attracted several pair of purple martins to our house. One particular pair has begun their nesting routine. During this routine, I observed the male and female taking turns retrieving material to construct their nest. It seemed as though one would stay and safeguard the home while the other went out searching for pine needles, leaves, grass clippings, mud or some other material for their nest. When one arrived with materials, the other would leave in search of some more. It was team work at its best. Such care and concern for the construction of their home and what seemed like instinctual behavior to work together. Each of them understood their role and was willing to fulfill their part of the bargain in the construction of their home.

Just this past weekend, I observed something that I had never seen purple martins do before. I was out on the patio watching and observing. Our bird house has a small tubular perch that stretches across the peak of the roof. One of the male martins had positioned himself on the extreme edge of one end of the perch. He wasn't making any noise, he wasn't pruning, he was just sitting there chilling out. It was about thirty minutes later that one of the females flew up to the bird house and was kind of buzzing around chirping like crazy. Are all you guys wondering as you read if there is a marriage lesson there? We won't go there! After a few more fly-by's the female found a spot on the perch at the extreme opposite end where the male had positioned himself. She sat quietly for a few moments, but then turned directly toward the male and started bursting out with more chirping and singing. The male just sat there, not even acknowledging any of her activity (ladies, this is not a marriage lesson either!). Out of no where, the female turned to face the male and began pecking the roof of the bird house, as though she was trying to get his attention. It didn't work. He just sat there, silent and uninterested in all of the commotion. After some time, she scooted closer to him on the perch and began pecking the roof some more. Again, despite her persistence, he just sat there undaunted. This process continued until she was almost right on top of him, pecking the roof in front of him and behind him. Unfortunately, it was about that time that I had to leave, so I never observed what finally happened. My last observation while I left was the male bird just sitting on the perch oblivious to all the activity and excitement being initiated from the female bird.

While the events I described above were unfolding, I invited my wife to come out and watch with me. She sat down beside me for a few minutes and watched the events progress for a while. It wasn't until later in the day that God brought these events back to my mind. He used what I simply observed in nature as an analogy to spiritual health. This same type of behavior takes place in the lives of Christians all over America. Upon the moment of their salvation, they take great care and concern toward their relationship with Jesus Christ. They tidy up their heart and are more than willing to do their part to develop an intimate relationship with Jesus. At that point, the Christian is definitely *it*, and they are chasing God with all their might. In those early days, there is an eagerness that consumes the new convert to do all they can in order to get their lives in line with God's Word and His will for their lives. This scenario follows the pattern of the male martin that instinctively seemed to do his best to help find a house and then tirelessly help construct a home. A funny thing seems to happen as time goes by. Inevitably, something happens after a period of time that tends to dampen the new converts enthusiasm. The initial emotion of a life set free from sin and those feelings of overwhelming acceptance tend to dissipate. It is in this moment that we realize we still have to live amongst the realities of this world and have to deal with the reality of temptation. Nothing has changed in the heart or mind of God, but we allow the business of life to overwhelm and confuse us.

The reality is that at this point in the progression of a relationship with God, some decide to push forward with their salvation experience and continue to pursue the relationship, while others will become mesmerized by the worlds distractions and settle for something far less than what God ever intended. Their pursuit of God flounders in the same way the emotional feelings did. There is an enormous rush initially, but the hum-drum details of everyday life beats down the enthusiasm and the feelings that come along with it. Unfortunately, when you live life by the way you feel, you will always be disappointed. The same is true when you base your Christian walk with the Lord on your feelings, you will often become discouraged. Of course while those feelings are real, the truth of the matter is that we are over-comes and are able to do *all things* through Christ Jesus.

Every Christian will face moments of discouragement and despair! For many, that moment may come in the form of criti-cism of their new found faith from unsaved friends or family members. For others, it may consummate when they began to compromise their conscience and return to their old ways, some-how thinking they're missing out on all the fun. For yet others, it will be because they figured they could just coast for a while. They assumed all the hard work had been done. Like the male martin, they sit in a dazed state, ignoring the call of God on their heart and His conviction of their conscience. One way or another it becomes easy to find an excuse to stop being *it* and stop chasing God and their spirit man slips into unconscious-ness. The expectation is that God will do all the work and we can just put our life and relationship with Him on auto-pilot. The Bible acknowledges that there are going to be seasons of weariness; "so don't get tired of doing what is good. Don't get discouraged and give up…" (Galatians 6:9, NLT). It's great to know that we have a God that not only knows we will face these kinds of feelings, but that he empathizes as well. I encourage you to hang on to these types of scriptures when you begin to experi-ence moments of discouragement and despair.

BUY NOW, PAY LATER

The events of today strike fear into the hearts of most. When analyzed at a local, national and global level, it all points to one thing from a Biblical perspective: the end times are drawing near. If you've grown up in church, you've probably heard about this for a very long time. I remember when I was in fifth grade, I was sitting in my Sunday School class when our well meaning teacher wrongly informed us that Jesus was coming back in 1979. He spoke with great conviction and was thoroughly convinced of what he was saying. I have to admit, he certainly convinced me too! In my eleven year old fragile and impressionable mind, I began to live in my own little terror filled world. I knew I loved God, but I also knew that I often wasn't living like I loved Him. As 1979 approached, I was constantly at the altar, trying to do everything I could to somehow appease God and make Him happy with me. I'm a little older now and a little wiser too. What I have come to understand is this: when we become performance driven in our relationship with God, most of the time it is because of our own insecurity in our relationship with God! We come to the conclusion that the more we do, the better chance we have at being accepted by God. When you follow this line of thinking, it produces a religious person who is committed to rituals, routines and duties. What we should want it a relationship with God through Jesus Christ that is based on submission and obedience.

There is nothing we can do that would be enough to pay for our salvation. Paul said it best, "God saved you by his special favor when you believed. And you can't take credit for this; it is a gift from God. Salvation is not a reward for the good things we have done, so none of us can boast about it." (Ephesians 2:8–9, NLT) When the American culture learns something is free, the immediate response is to try and take advantage of it. The inclination of the American heart is to take advantage of God's forgiveness, grace and love. We find the answer to this attitude in the scripture as well, "should we keep on sinning so that God can show us more and more kindness and forgiveness? Of course not! Since we have died to sin, how can we continue to live in it?" (Romans 6:1–2, NLT)

During this period of turmoil, as an eleven-year-old, each time I found myself alone, my mind began to wander. Even as a young boy, I would wonder if I had missed the trumpet blast signaling the end times. I lived in the terror of the unexpected but definite return of Jesus Christ. I hate to admit this now, but on several occasions, during a panic stricken moment, I would call people that I thought in my mind were "holy." I went so far as to develop a mental hierarchy, ranking friends and relatives based on their spiritual prowess. When things got bad, I would call the person on the top of my mental super-Christian list. I placed a phone call and there was no answer. That weight in the pit of my stomach grew heavier, and I proceeded to the next person on the list. I did this until I got an answer on the other end. As soon as I found someone that answered, I would quickly hang up! Based on how far down the list I had to go before I got an answer, sometimes I felt better and other times it did nothing to settle me. The further down on the list I had to go, the less confident I felt. Maybe I had misjudged their spirituality. It wasn't until I was physically able to make contact with one of the top members of the hierarchy that I could relax. I am grateful the phone companies had not come up with some the capabilities we have today like caller-id or call return, when I was eleven. That sure saved me a lot of embarrassment.

The hidden danger in this type of behavior is that familiarity often breeds contempt. My fear was that something was going to happen. Fortunately for me, it didn't. As time went on the fear came and the panic set in, but nothing resulted. Alarms were sounding in my mind, but there was never a fire. We've all heard the story of the boy that cried wolf. With each cry for help, those that heard him cry became desensitized to his plea. It was the same cry for help that was ignored in the end because the audience had become used to hearing the same old story over and over without the actual event occurring. This similar set of circumstances in my life paved the way for years of rebellion and disillusionment with God when I was a teenager.

Many have heard the story of the second coming of our Lord time and time again. They read books like currently popular "Left Behind" series and think of it all as some cute make believe story. No one knows exactly how those events will unfold, but to dismiss the actual event because they are referred to in a fictional set of novels would be ludicrous. Unfortunately, many dismiss this series are strictly fictional but are somehow drawn to believe in other printed material based on the exciting nature of the material.

Take a look at what America is reading. According to a recent article in the Miami herald, the top five best selling books in the fiction category, according to the Wall Street Journal, were:[5]

1. *The Da Vinci Code* by Dan Brown (Doubleday)

2. *The Rule of Four* by Ian Caldwell and Dustin Thomason (Dial Books)

3. *Five People You Meet in Heaven* by Mitch Albom (Hyperion)

4. *Oh, the Places You'll Go!* Dr. Seuss (Random House)

5. *Angels & Demons* by Dan Brown (Atria)

Three of these top five books relate to the Bible, some form of divinity, or Christian history in one way or another. One of the main thrusts of *The Da Vinci Code* is to denounce the Bible as an accurate literary source. It implies that Jesus was married to Mary Magdalene and the early church simply tried to cover it all up. Of course, the genre of the book is fiction, which means it is not supposed to be considered factual. Fiction is, by the very definition of the word, an imaginative creation that is not based on actual events. The author, however, is more than happy to present his sensationalized fiction as though it is factual. The problem, it seems, is that some people have taken the story to be true. Brown has encouraged this confusion by insisting upon the book's historical accuracy. It does appear that there are some accurate historical facts. The problem is they are placed alongside falsehoods and other made up or misleading statements. Any time you combine something true with something false, the whole thing has to be considered false. Further:

> "Brown has argued that historical arguments are themselves suspect because history is written 'by those societies and belief systems that conquered and survived.' This is a cop-out. It is disingenuous for Brown to present his book as factual and then hide behind questions like 'how historically accurate is history itself?'"[6]

Brown's other novel, *Angels and Demons,* came in at number five. This one pits scientific terrorists against the cardinals of Vatican City. It is simply a swipe at Christian history. Brown implies sinister dealings amongst the early founders of the church.

Coming in at number three is, *The Five People You Meet in Heaven.* This fictional novel follows an elderly man that dies on his eighty-third birthday. The premise is:

> "He awakes in the afterlife, where he learns that heaven is not a destination, but rather a place where your life is explained to you by five people, some of whom you knew, others who may have been strangers. These five people are waiting to show him the true meaning and value of his life. One by one, these mostly unexpected characters remind him that we all live in a vast web of interconnection with other lives; that all our stories overlap; that acts of sacrifice seemingly small or fruitless do affect others; and that loyalty and love matter to a degree we can never fathom. Heaven is simply the place where you find understanding for your life on earth."[7]

Sounds like a cute story, which is exactly the problem. Even the title implies that you will make it to heaven. The book likely would not have done as well in sales had it been called "Five people you meet if you make it to heaven." Once the conditions to actually making it to heaven are removed from the equation, it becomes more appeasing to the minds of Americans. Too many authors try to sell their modern day literature as factual. They use their role as a writer as a source of influence. Most people assume that writers must know everything about what they write about. That is simply not true. While there is a lot of research and work that goes into writing a book, you should never give an author carte blanche in terms of knowledge of a subject matter.

As people read this type of material, they begin to ask themselves things like "will I really meet five people when I go to heaven?" The natural progression is then to begin to entertain statements in their mind like "I guess so, because everyone will end up in heaven anyway." You can see why today's society is so confused about what the truth really is and what it is not. A recent report in *USA Today* indicated that "fiction, led by thrillers, staged a comeback, accounting for 72% of last year's weekly best sellers, compared with 59% in 1998."[8] More and more America is reading fiction, allowing the fascination of literary creation to shape their perception of reality. The best sellers highlighted above offer opinions that contradict the teachings of the Bible. When those opinions are held as fact in the minds of readers, those readers view the Bible as just a bunch of fictional stories and opinions.

THE FACT

Paul told Timothy that in the last days men would be lovers of themselves and their money.

> "You should also know this, Timothy, that in the last days there will be very difficult times. For people will love only themselves and their money. They will be boastful and proud, scoffing at God, disobedient to their parents, and ungrateful. They will consider nothing sacred. They will be unloving and unforgiving; they will slander others and have no self-control; they will be cruel and have no interest in what is good. They will betray their friends, be reckless, be puffed up with pride, and love pleasure rather than God. They will act as if they are religious, but they will reject the power that could make them godly. You must stay away from people like that"

> (2 Timothy 3:1–5, NLT)

That, my friends, is a description of where America is today. The majority in America, Christians included, have a self-satis-fying and self-serving mentality. We have become a society that seeks pleasure and convenience at every corner. It is a society that wants nothing to do with righteousness and holiness, but wants to be seen as spiritual sound. The conveniences of modern day technology have helped us develop an attitude that we must have whatever it is we want, exactly when we want it. That mentality of immediate gratification has transformed both the way American Christians perceive God and the expectations they put on God. Unless something makes life easier, brings pleasure or totally conforms to my way of thinking, then it is not for me. If it means I have to change or work harder or be inconvenienced, then forget it! Unfortunately, the American Church is not doing enough to shape the mentality of our society. Too many churches become exclusionary, judgmental and self-serving, which is the opposite of the way things should be.

This didn't catch God by surprise though, He knew this would be the case. He actually warned us of this very situation when John wrote to the lukewarm church of Laodicea in the book of Revelation:

"I know all the things you do, that you are neither hot nor cold. I wish you were one or the other! But since you are like lukewarm water, I will spit you out of my mouth! You say, 'I am rich. I have everything I want. I don't need a thing!' And you don't realize that you are wretched and miserable and poor and blind and naked. I advise you to buy gold from Me—gold that has been purified by fire. Then you will be rich. And also buy white garments so you will not be shamed by your nakedness. And buy ointment for your eyes so you will be able to see. I am the one who corrects

and disciplines everyone I love. Be diligent and turn from
your indifference"

(Revelation 3:15–19, NLT)

These words were spoken to a church, not just some bunch of
randomly gathered people. It addresses a church that had allowed
themselves to slip into thinking they had reached some spiritual
milestone. They considered themselves amongst the spiritual
elite. In reaching that pinnacle, they forgot the main principle of
Christianity that Jesus so beautifully portrayed for us in person:
humility. In order to be the greatest, you must be willing to be a
servant to all! This message is still being spoken into the hearts
of those that are willing to listen for His voice. Unfortunately,
if you are not willing to listen, you won't even realize that you
haven't heard Him.

The church at Laodicea was convinced they were on the
right track. It was their self-sufficiency, self-righteousness and
arrogance that led Christ to say what He did. Warren Wiersbe
remarked, "These people couldn't see themselves as they really
were. Nor could they see God as He stood outside the door of
the church. Nor could they see the open door of opportunity.
They were so wrapped up in building their own kingdom that
they had become lukewarm in their concern for a lost world and
the things of God."[9]

Today's church and today's Christian are often more interested in self-preservation than in reaching the lost. The mentality that the church exists to meet *my* needs is not what the first
century apostles taught, nor is it what Jesus had in mind. Christians today won't admit it or say it in those terms, but the actions
and activities they involve themselves in speak much louder than
their words. "Americans are spiritually lukewarm. 'Very limited
effort is devoted to spiritual growth. Most Americans experi-

ence 'accidental spiritual growth' since there is generally no plan or process other than showing up at a church and absorbing a few ideas here and there. Even then, few people have a defined understanding of what they are hoping to become, as followers of Christ.' Barna attributed much of this to the numerous distractions common in most people's lives."[10]

Just think of your church, or even of your own personal life and think of the last time you saw someone saved. Whether it was because of the ministry of your church or the testimony of your life, when was the last time you saw someone come to know Jesus Christ as their personal savior? "Evangelism is not a priority in most churches, so the fact that most churched adults do not verbally share the gospel in a given year is not deemed problematic."[11]

When was the last time you attended a prayer meeting? When was the last time you saw more than five percent of your church attend a prayer meeting together? The church in America at large doesn't pray. If pastors around America called a prayer meeting this week, they would be lucky to draw ten percent of their congregation. Of course, the smaller the church, the easier it is to get a large percentage. If you were to get two out of a congregation of twenty, that is really no better than two-hundred out of a congregation of two-thousand. Some churches may be able to draw as much as twenty-five percent, but the median would likely fall between five and ten percent. Call the same prayer meeting at a church overseas and you would see numbers that are nearly reverse. More people would show up than those that would not!

America is not interested in sacrifice. Sacrifice is required for personal holiness. Personal holiness is required for revival. Too many are not willing to pay the price or put forth a legitimate effort. "Holiness is a matter embraced by the Christian Church, but it is not one that many Americans adopt as a focal point of their faith development. This is partially because barely one-third of Americans (thirty-five percent) contend that 'God expects you to become holy.' A larger share of the born again public believes God has called them to holiness (forty-six percent) but that portion remains a minority of the born again population.[12]"

The process of how a Christian gets to the point where prayer and holiness are expendable is what I like to call spiritual slippage. It's not usually an overnight process. It's likely not even a process that is noticeable, especially if it is happening to you. It's a gradual process. You don't figure out everything you need to know on your first day of school, it is a gradual process of education that allows you to learn and gain intelligence. As you slip spiritually, it is manifested by gradually replacing spiritual activity with things more in line with your old habits and lifestyle.

Believe it or not, most farmers are smarter than most Christians. It used to be that farmers would plow under the previous year's crop stubble, burying it by churning the top layers of soil. In recent years, no-till farming has become the standard practice. With this method, crop stubble is left after harvest instead of plowed under. This process actually helps prevent the loss of fertile topsoil, thus maximizing dirt and moisture retention. Farmers realized the loss of the fertile topsoil is a detriment to crop health and growth. Likewise, the loss of time-tested principles to the soil of your soul will stunt your spiritual growth.

THE MISSING INGREDIENT

I like to bake. I've developed a personal recipe for cheesecake that some say is the best they have ever tasted. Ok, at least my wife and kids say that. When you bake a cake without a specific but seemingly insignificant ingredient, that cake just doesn't taste right. If you forget that teaspoon of vanilla extract, your cake is going to taste funny.

One of the missing ingredients in American society today is that of personal responsibility. It is a fact that there are often consequences for our decisions and actions. In the mind of most, everything is always someone else's fault. No one wants to take responsibility for their actions. Of those that may admit a fault, they expect there to be no punishment or consequences for their behavior. After all, isn't being sorry enough? They interpret punishment as someone picking on them. They think that no one likes them or that everyone has a biased opinion about them.

When Saul made the choice to destroy the Gibeonites because they aggravated him, he did not seek God's counsel or look to Him for direction. He leaned on the wisdom of his counselors. Because of his action, there was a price to pay. In this case, the price would be a very steep one. The consequence was that seven of his sons were put to death. Any step taken in the wrong direction by a Christian can be forgiven by God, but there may be some consequences as well.

We have somehow come to expect and assume that once a wrong move has been made, all they need to do is simply to confess the mistake and seek forgiveness from God. This certainly is the first step. This is the action required in order to receive God's forgiveness. However, it does not always eliminate the consequences for our actions as we just mentioned. It also does not always remove the feelings of guilt that often permeate our minds. This is one of the devil's single most effective points of attack. He loves to remind us of what we have done wrong in the past. He loves to show us our past offenses against God. He will constantly remind you of why you are not good enough. At the moment of confession and sincere repentance, the sin is forgiven. At that point, God chooses not to remember it anymore. Whenever our past is brought to our remembrance, you can be assured it's not God's fault!

If, in a moment of weak faith, we commit sin or are enticed and deceived by our enemy, God's Word assures us that we can be forgiven. As we go about working through the resulting consequences of our sin, it may very well cause us grief or difficulty. Sometimes it may be brief while at other times it may last a lifetime. Only God's grace allows for forgiveness of our willful wrong choices; only His mercy restores all that comes from our rash compromise with evil. We are totally dependent on Him providing it for us and there is nothing we can do to *earn* it.

Because you are not the one in control, the philosophy of the world says this is a position of weakness. Weakness is not a trait that is looked on with favor by our American culture. In fact, the world frowns on weakness while God embraces it. God is in fact attracted to weakness, because in that weakness, He can receive the glory and honor for whatever takes place. Pride is the great sin of man, the one that started this whole mess. When Adam and Eve chose to believe that God could be wrong, they penned the very definition of what pride is: I think I'm right when I may be wrong. Pride is the enemy of humility and the adversary of servant hood. It will initiate spiritual slippage and ultimately lead to your spiritual demise. Humility is the great spiritual healer. In humility we find our dependence on God is in fact not weakness, but rather is His unlimited strength at our disposal.

THE NEED FOR DEPENDENCE

Think for a minute about the way our westernized culture approaches dating and romantic relationships. When you think about it, they usually begin with at least some measure of fraud and deception. What a sad way to begin a relationship. We tell each other what we think they want to hear. We try to be what we think they want us to be. All of this is done without ever inquiring as to whether or not our opinions of what they want to hear or what they want us to be are correct!

Admit it, when you first met your husband or wife you were definitely out to impress them. You would inconvenience yourself to please them. It's no wonder that when we suddenly wake up and return to being more our self, that we become disenchanted and frustrated with each other. In those initial stages of the relationship, there is a whirlwind of attention, unabated romance and intimate communication. There were times when I was dating my wife that we would spend hours on the phone, talking about everything. As time went on, as we became accustomed to the everyday stuff, things began to change. Romance faded and the everyday task of relational maintenance kicked into gear. We got used to eating at the same time, we had kids and patterns developed that brought schedule and routine to our daily lives. There is nothing wrong with schedule and routine, but it has a tendency to zap any inkling of spontaneity and romance from a relationship. You also begin to uncover each others faults and weaknesses. In those early days of the relationship, you'd leave work early just to spend that ten extra minutes with the one you love. As time goes by, you try to leave home ten minutes early so you can get out of the house before your spouse wakes up and gives you some sort of to do list. You can't place the blame on any one of the two parties involved, because the blame is divided equally between both parties involved in the relationship.

There are two main reasons for frustration in relationships. First is the disillusionment of trying to change each other. Second is the emptiness that is left when we have unmet expectations. All too often, the expectations are never even vocalized to the other. This creates an atmosphere that is both unfair and unrealistic. All of this leads to distance in the relationship that shows up through lack of intimate communication, forced romance and being taken for granted.

FEELINGS

Marriages that are built on the foundation of feelings will crumble when the first difficulties come along. Marriage is actually a commitment between three people. The first two involved are pretty obvious, the husband and the wife. The third person is God. I doubt anyone enters a marriage without definite feelings of love. Relational experiences with others can bring a variety of overwhelming emotional feelings. Any relationship built in anticipation of that emotional surge continuing is in store for inevitable disappointment. If there is no provision for the absence of high emotional feelings in the relationship, when tough times come, there is nothing to lean on.

All of these aspects of romantic relationships are true in our relationship with our savior. When our relationship is based on emotion and feelings, we somehow think God has left us in the cold when certain feelings are absent. Hopefully you do not only love your spouse when you are in a good mood or feel good. No doubt you love them in good times and bad! In terms of our relationship with God, He owes us nothing. He already gave everything He had when He sent His Son to die for our sins. If you treat God as though He owes you something, you really have no desire or intention of building a relationship with Him. That type of attitude sucks the very life out of any relationship. With that type of attitude, there is no real desire to fulfill your responsibilities in the relationship.

BACK TO THE BIRDS

I want to get back to the story about purple martins for a minute. We were fortunate enough to have one of the mature pairs successfully breed and lay six eggs. I meticulously monitored the progress of the incubation period and the subsequent growth of the youngsters.

Purple Martin Eggs

Purple Martin Babies

The young birds were totally dependent on their parents for their every need. It is amazing the way the parents wore themselves out all day long, flying back and forth with various insects to feed the youngsters. The little ones would make all kinds of noise, especially when the parents came around. Instinctually, the young birds knew their parents were going to bring them food. They didn't have to stand around and try to determine if what their parents had brought was what they wanted. No, they knew that whatever it was, it was going to be good for them. Actually, the reaction of the young birds was always as if what the parents brought was exactly what they needed. That is exactly how our relationship with God should be. We need to be totally dependent on Him. We shouldn't examine the things God brings our way to see if we want to partake in them or if we're going to pass on them this time. God will only give us good things, exactly the things we need!

A very unfortunate incident occurred shortly after the fledglings were approaching the age to be able to fly on their own.

Two of the youngsters had already successfully made their first flight. My two sons were playing in the back yard and ran into the steel pole on which the bird house is erected. Purple Martins prefer to nest as high as possible. My pole has a three section telescoping mechanism that allows it to reach heights around twenty-five to thirty feet. The boys were fine (they have hard heads), but the shock of the movement sent all the birds scurrying out of the house. For the remaining four youngsters, this event marked their first flight. None of the four had a particularly successful first flight! One landed in nearby trees and stayed there for some time. Two others fluttered around enough to be able to finally get back to roost on the top of the bird house. The last of the four was found, later that night, just sitting on my back porch. I was able to get a hold of him (he flapped around a lot and took short spurts in the air), lowered the pole and inserted the youngster back into one of the available holes. The poor little guy looked like he should be able to take off on his own and survive. Every one of the other youngsters was hatched within hours of one another. All the others had successfully made it back to their home on their own. It would lead one to believe that this one bird should have been able to do and be all the things that the others were. However, with birds, just as with people, that is not a fair judgment to make. We can not try to fly on our own before we are ready. We can not compare ourselves to others. Our relationship with God must be thought of as a lifetime achievement. It has a definite beginning here on earth, but the ending point is after your life on earth is over. Our pursuit of God and the maturing process to be like Jesus is what the dash will represent on our tombstones. We can do nothing about the day we are born and nothing about the day we die. The only part of the process we can affect is the dash.

TIME TO WAIT

As with everything else, we grow inpatient with any process that isn't going according to our plans. In our impatience, we loose sight of the fact that any amount of waiting is never in vain. You can't grow a flower any faster by worrying about it. You can't make time go by any faster by getting frustrated. Things take time. Growing takes time. James compared waiting on God like this: "Consider the farmers who eagerly look for the rains in the fall and in the spring. They patiently wait for the precious harvest to ripen. You, too, must be patient. And take courage, for the coming of the Lord is near" (James 5:7b-8, NLT).

Waiting on God does not mean you have resigned yourself to have no real useful future. It doesn't mean that you have become idle. There are always things we must do. That time we often consider a waste is often God's way of preparing us for what is coming next. Preparation is a necessary prerequisite to make productive and fruitful progress. You would not trust your child to drive without first having had some form of formal training, oversight and multiple hours of driving in safe and restricted conditions under the supervision of a responsible adult. Don't expect God to disclose and fulfill His perfect will for your lifetime in the first year of your Christian walk. Do what you know to do and let God teach you what to do next. Like the farmer, we work and wait for God to bring forth the fullness of His answer over time. There will be days of stillness and there will be days of labor. Both are necessary.

The main motivation to persist in times of waiting is the knowledge that God is actively preparing our hearts to receive the right answer at the right time. The waiting is never in vain. The process God is taking you through will make you stronger. The outcome will ultimately bring glory to His name.

Many of you, I am sure, have experienced those uneasy feelings that accompany making a quick decision. Once it is made, we walk away and wonder whether or not we did the right thing. Often there is a nagging sense of doubt that we should have waited rather than make a decision at all. Is this type of feeling avoidable? Certainly it is. There is always the potential for some measure of doubt, but it is often centered in our own insecurity. We have to learn both how and when to wait on God. You must have confidence in God's direction as He leads you, as difficult as it seems at the time. Patience and waiting are not prevailing characteristics of the American culture. As I mentioned before, our society uses cell-phones, faxes, email and overnight mail services as a standard way of life. We are immediately accessible to others with the touch of a few buttons. In all actuality, God is just as accessible. The problem is in our ability to spiritually hear. In my experience, God only answers prayer in three ways: Yes, No and Wait.

Too often, we ignore God when His response is to wait. I can certainly admit to being guilty of that. I imagine that almost every one of us has made the mistake of pushing ahead of Him in the decision-making process. Bad decisions have consequences. The worst mistake you can make is to fail to wait for God's timing. As I mentioned earlier, God always has our best in mind. He will deliver, in His time. Instead of considering it an annoyance when the answer is to wait, try considering it a blessing. After all, He is stopping you from making a concrete decision. Maybe there is something else you need to understand before you make this decision. Maybe you just aren't ready for the answer. He may very well be saving you from physical and emotional pain! There are an infinite number of reasons why God would want us to wait. God uses the time you spend waiting to prepare you for the future. You never really have to worry about missed opportunities because when the timing is right, God will open the right doors. Just be sure you keep on knocking!

The idea is to remain pliable, moldable and changeable to God's will and plan. As change will be intended to help you grow, growth will always bring the need to change. Jeremiah made this same allusion in chapter 18 of his book.

> Go down to the shop where clay pots and jars are made. I will speak to you while you are there.' So I did as he told me and found the potter working at his wheel. But the jar he was making did not turn out as he had hoped, so the potter squashed the jar into a lump of clay and started again.
>
> (Jeremiah 18:2–4, NLT)

Once the jar is formed and put in the fire, the only way to bring about change is to destroy it. During the forming of the jar, the potter has the luxury of molding and shaping it at will. It's never easy to be stretched, but it is certainly easier than being destroyed and starting from scratch! When we become rigid and set in our ways we become as a jar that has hardened from the finishing process. Any change from that point is going to be extremely painful. When you allow the time, effort and changing to happen on the front-end of the process, it is certainly not easy, but much less painful than the alternative. Remain open and flexible to God's plan.

In a society where immediacy has become the standard and patience is a lost art form, Christians must be careful not to be influenced by their culture. Instead, they should constantly be looking for opportunities to affect the ways in which their community, city and culture thinks. Christians need not be afraid to take a stand and make a difference. What they should fear is compromising and giving in to what everyone else is doing.

American culture preaches tolerance for everything, freedom for everyone and independence from anything! God says that you need to fully and wholly depend on Him for everything you need. Keep an open mind and an open eye to ways in which you can begin to influence others rather than allowing them to influence you! Revolutionize your perspective of how powerful the affect and influence of the world has become on your own life. It will take a paradigm shift, a change in the ways you think. We must, however, recover the ground that has been given up. We must restore the areas of our minds that the world has managed to corrupt.

PARADIGM SHIFT

I'm always amazed by the simplicity of the life that Jesus lived. Don't get me wrong, I know that life is never always simple. There are always good days and bad days. When I look at the life of Jesus, He exhibited greatness in everything He did. In a way, He made life look simple. He had a perspective of life the way it should be and that made it look to be fairly simple. In His mind, all the twists and turns that His life took were simply opportunities to glorify His Father. For you and me, it certainly will not seem that way while in the middle of a difficult situation! There are times when you will be stronger and more resilient than others. Rather than expecting God to immediately remove your difficulty and make everything better, begin to examine your attitude and response to difficulty while you are in the middle of it. That is not how the world thinks! The world tells you to go ahead and get married, if it doesn't turn out like *you* want it to; you can always abandon the marriage and get rid of the problem. We've been so bombarded that some Christians have come to accept this type of thinking as well. We need to get back to thinking and acting like Jesus. Christians today need to change the way they look at things.

CHANGE THE WAY YOU THINK

Instead of always looking out for number one, start considering others instead of yourself. After all, that is the exact advice that Paul gave the church at Philippi. The world looks out for themselves above everything and everyone else. The world is selfish. The world thinks their needs are more important than anyone or anything else. How about you?

Too many Christians today have very thin skin. Their feelings are hurt too easily. They change churches like they change clothes, trying to get rid of their problem. Too many want to blame everything and everyone else for their problems. They fail to seem the common denominator in all of their issues is… themselves! This has to change. It must change. Gene Edwards wrote a book that conveys the story of Saul and David. It relates the methods David used to respond to Saul torments. Gene wrote:

David had a question: What do you do when someone throws a spear at you?

Does it seem odd to you that David did not know the answer to this question? After all, everyone else in the world knows what to do when a spear is thrown at you. Why, you pick up the spear and throw it right back!

When someone throws a spear at you, David, just wrench it out of the wall and throw it right back. Everyone else does, you can be sure.

And in performing this small feat of returning thrown spears, you will prove many things: You are courageous. You stand for the right. You boldly stand against the wrong. You are tough and can't be pushed around. You will not stand for injustice or unfair treatment. You are a defender of the faith, keeper of the flame detector of all heresy. You will not be wronged. All these attributes then combine to prove that you are also a candidate for kingship. Yes, perhaps you are the Lord's anointed.

After the order of King Saul.

There is also a possibility that some twenty years after your coronation, *you will be the most incredibly skilled spear thrower in the realm. And also by then...*

Quite mad.

Unlike anyone else in spear-throwing history, David did not know what to do when a spear was thrown at him. He did not throw Sauls spear back at him. Nor did he make any spears of his own and throw them. Something was different about David. All he did was dodge the spears.

What can a man, especially a young man, do when the king decides to use him for target practice? What if the young man decides not to return the compliment?

First of all, he must pretend he cannot see spears. Even when they are coming straight at him. Second, he must learn to duck very quickly. Last, he must pretend nothing happened.

You can easily tell when someone has been hit by a spear. He turns a deep shade of bitter. David never got hit. Gradually, he learned a very well-kept secret. He discovered three things that prevented him from ever being hit.

One, never learn anything about the fashionable, easily mastered art of spear throwing. Two, stay out of the company of spear throwers. And three, keep your mouth tightly closed.

In this way, spears will never touch you, even when they pierce your heart.[B]

What a simple way to explain the need to see God's hand in the midst of difficulty. We all need to learn not to immediately dismiss God's hand in a situation when it doesn't fit into our preconceived plan for our lives. It is easy to be blinded by the anger that has developed from finding yourself in the midst of difficulty. When you struggle and fight to get out of your situation instead of taking time to understand what God is saying, you are in effect saying you know what is best for your own life. That type of attitude says you know what is best, so God must not know what He is doing! It is in the prayer for a quick and short way out of your difficulty that you circumvent what God has orchestrated to bring the spiritual growth He has in mind for you. When you circumvent what God has in mind, He will find another, perhaps even more painful avenue by which to teach you the same lesson down the road.

CHANGE THE WAY YOU ACT

I have learned to base a lot of my earthly relationship from the idea that people don't care how much you know until they know how much you care. Consider the depth of that statement for a minute. Think of how it relates to the life of a Christian. Think of how it relates to the teaching of James in James 2:14–16:

> Dear friends, do you think you'll get anywhere in this if you learn all the right words but never do anything? Does merely talking about faith indicate that a person really has it? For instance, you come upon an old friend dressed in rags and half-starved and say, 'Good morning, friend! Be clothed in Christ! Be filled with the Holy Spirit!' and walk off without providing so much as a coat or a cup of soup - where does that get you?

(James 2:14–16, MSG)

It is very easy to use your mouth to form words that sound wonderful but really don't cost you anything. It is a much more costly commitment to actually roll your sleeves up and get into the middle of things. It says so much more to someone when you actually put your life on hold in order to serve them.

Ted Haggard has much to say about this subject. In fact, some of his writing has revolutionized the way I think about a lot of things. He refers to two approaches to living life—from the perspective of the tree of the knowledge of good and evil or from the perspective of the tree of life. Living in the tree of life means making choices that will lead to life—in our lives and in the lives of those around us. Living in the tree of the knowledge of good and evil means making choices based on what is good and what is evil—which leads to death in us and possibly to those around us.[14]

I have encountered countless people, unfortunately most of them in churches, that are intensely legalistic, incredibly religious and consumed with being right. In fact, they are more consumed with being right than doing right! For way too long, denominations have been pitted against one another and theologians have argued to the point of exclusion of one another. There have been attempts to set aside differences and move forward as though on the same team, but there needs to be more consistency in order to bring glory to the kingdom of God.

Another tree of the knowledge of good and evil issue is the church's opinion of sinners. I am amazed at how many exhibit an elitist, religious mindset that looks down on others. I knew a pastor's wife that was appalled when teenage girls would come to church dressed inappropriately. Of course, the fact that it was that teenager girls first time ever darkening the doors of a church did not seem to matter much to her. Teenagers at that church were afraid to invite their unsaved friends from school; for fear that someone may say something about what they were wearing. Instead of a tree of the knowledge of good and evil attitude that judged them based on their appearance, why not take the tree of life approach and be full of love and acceptance toward sinners that have been brave enough to come to church? Why be consumed with changing who they are and how they look? Isn't that God's job anyway? Would you rather sinners not come to your church so that your rules regarding appropriate church behavior and attire remain intact? Sinners are supposed to act like sinners because that is what they are. You do not expect your dog to meow and your cat to bark so do not put unrealistic expectations on those that have not come to know Christ yet either! On the other hand, Christians are supposed to act like Christ. They should operate in the same unconditional love, unconditional acceptance and unconditional forgiveness that Jesus did. If you can genuinely embrace these qualities, people from all walks of life will be attracted to you!

I can not resist one last admonishment to church leaders everywhere. If your church is growing predominantly due to transfer growth, you may be suffering from a tree of the knowledge of good and evil mindset. Those that transfer from church to church are made up of what I have determined to be two categories. First are the job-hoppers. These are legitimate changes in vocation or location that cause the need to find a new church. Second are the church-hoppers. These are the ones that have become dissatisfied or disenchanted with their old church leadership and have determined there must be a church out there that sees everything the way they do. They have all the answers as to why everything is wrong with everyone else, but have conveniently chosen to exclude themselves from that list. It's only a matter of time before the church-hoppers that show up in your church will become dissatisfied or disenchanted with the leadership at their new church and move on again. Every church will naturally experience some transfer growth, but it must be coupled with a healthy influx of conversion growth to remain balanced and vibrant.

LOVE COVERS A MULTITUDE OF SIN

An important tree of life principle I try to impress on people is that you can only change yourself. When you try to change others, you are often met with resistance. Concentrate on changing yourself and leave the job of changing others to the Holy Spirit and His convicting power! In time, as they listen to God's voice, they will begin to change on their own.

Those that try to change others often battle with anger, bitterness or unforgiveness in their own life. I find the same is true of those who take on others personal offenses. When a friend is offended and you choose to take their side of the offense, you are asking for trouble. Often unknowingly, you pass judgment on others by deciding who is right and who is wrong. Remember how Adam and Eve reacted after they ate from the tree of the knowledge of good and evil? They blamed someone else! The denial of personal responsibility started early in our history, but we have certainly learned how to perfect it!

The Bible describes love as being able to cover a multitude of sin. That is not the type of love that most Christians operate in! They want someone to blame, someone to be right and someone to be wrong. They operate in the tree of the knowledge of good and evil rather than promoting acceptance, love and forgiveness by operating in the tree of life! Make the decision today to operate in the tree of life by changing not only the way you act, but the way you think.

STOP PRETENDING

Our reaction to life, the choices we make, are what end up defining who we really are. Our character defines who we are than anything else and there is a clear distinction between character and reputation. A man's reputation is what people think he is. A man's character is what God knows him to be. We live and operate in an image-conscious society. There is great emphasis on how we appear in the public eye. Everyone is concerned about their public *image*. There is little, if any, positive attention given to what we are in private. What a man is in private, in the eyes of God, is what ultimately matters.

Because of this social pressure, there's a tendency in Christians to develop separate public and private identities too. Keeping our "happy" face visible to everyone becomes a full-time job. We can't allow anyone to see us for who we really are and what we are going through. We can't bear the though that people will see our flaws, so we pretend to be perfect. It's crazy, but we've all done it. Remember that time you and your spouse were frustrated with each other on the way to church? Remember the words you used toward each other and the way you felt? That stuff happens to all of us. It's just normal life stuff. But when you recall what happened in the car, do you also remember what happened when you got out of the car? Do you remember shaking someone's hand? Do you remember when someone asked you how you were and you said "great!" Do you remember praying for those around you? Do you remember getting back in the car a few hours later, taking off your "happy" mask and returning to the real you? I'm sure your spouse does!

I'm certainly not trying to imply that you have to always wear all your emotions on your sleeve, but it is this "role playing" Christianity in America that has come to be a message of confusion to the lost. They see us act one way in public and then get caught acting another way in private. Often getting caught doing things that only serve to blur the differences between Christians and everyone else.

This isn't a new concept. Jesus had to deal with this type of behavior everywhere He went in His ministry. Jesus encountered the religious leaders of His day at every turn. They were called the Sadducees and Pharisees. Jesus often used the phrase hypocrites when referring to them. Fifteen times alone in the book of Matthew, Jesus addresses the religious leaders of His day with the term hypocrite. The meaning of this Hebrew/Greek word is quite enlightening: an actor, stage player, a pretender.[15] These religious leaders were always trying the look good on the outside but weren't that concerned about who they were on the inside.

Did you have to read *The Picture of Dorian Gray* by Oscar Wilde in high school? Remember the premise of the novel? Dorian Gray was the subject of a painting. He was selected because of his remarkable beauty. He came to believe the only thing worth pursuing in life was beauty, and the fulfillment of the senses. Knowing that one day his beauty would fade, Dorian makes what could be considered a deal with the devil. He made a wish that his portrait would age rather than himself. The portrait served as a reminder of the effect each act had upon his soul, with each sin being displayed as well as all the signs of aging.[16]

Dorian hid the portrait so no one would see it and was able to fool people for the rest of his life. As Christians, we can't have secret lives or hidden chambers where we try to hide our sin.

Just before Jesus left this earth, He left us with some words that we have come to know as the great commission. In those challenging words, Jesus called not only the Christians of that day, but everyone that would come to the knowledge that they need a savior to carry the message of the gospel forward. This life changing message is to be taken to every corner of the earth. To be honest, the American church is doing a pretty good job at carrying out that task. Meanwhile, America has become one of the largest and most difficult mission fields in the world. Leighton Ford says, "North America is now the largest mission field in the English-speaking world, and the third-largest after China and India. We are in a mission situation in our own country."[17] The North American Mission Board (NAMB) estimates that the lost population of the United States is two-hundred million, which equates to seventy percent of the total population.[18]

America is the new foreign mission field for the American church. Not only because of the American people has become a largely lost community, but also because the nations of the world are coming to America in record numbers. As they come, they bring their ethnicities, their cultures, their values, and their religions. They need to know the truth. They need hope. It's our responsibility to take the gospel to our local communities as well as across the world. Your community is out there waiting; you have to be willing to make the first move forward.

America grows more and more non-Christian, secular, and diverse with each passing day. In many ways, we are no longer a churched culture. While America is still considered to be a Christian community by most, those that call themselves Christian have become less and less involved in church (physically, financially and spiritually). If we hope to have any chance of capturing the hearts and minds of the next generation, things can not remain as they have.

A day of opportunity and great urgency is upon us all. To rise to these challenges, Christian leaders will have to make radical changes in their spiritual mind-sets and in their strategies. The church in America needs to stop playing games and get serious about living out the Christian life in victory as well as reaching the lost.

TAKING ACTION

Hopefully, you are now awake and your eyes are wide open. My prayer in the introduction of this book was that you not just nod your head in agreement with the words on the page and then go about your life, doing the same things you have always done; that would be insane. My desire is to do everything I can to assist you with the *get going* part! The problem most of us have is figuring out what to do once we finally realize something is wrong.

One of the first things we all need to do is be alert. So how do we do that? Peter told us in his gospel to be alert and vigilant. Why? Because our adversary, the devil, is roaming the earth, seeking someone to devour. We need to take that very seriously. Life is not a game. Spiritual warfare is not something you find in a fiction book or on a movie screen. In the mundane details of everyday life, never forget that your adversary is always lurking somewhere in the background, waiting for an opportunity to tempt and deceive you. To help you keep that in the forefront of your mind, make it a point to journal regarding your spiritual walk as often as possible. You should journal about your struggles, journal about your victories, journal about your prayers, and journal about answers to your prayers. Keeping a record like that will ignite your faith and keep you alert!

We also have to learn how to deal with forgiveness. Forgiveness isn't always easy, but that doesn't change the fact that we are responsible for extending forgiveness to others, whether we feel it is deserved or not. That's how God forgives us, so we have to do the same. It doesn't stop there, though. We also have to be willing to forgive *ourselves*. Remember that everyone makes mistakes. Even the most righteous person you know is not perfect! Remember, Christianity is a process, not an event. When (not if) you mess up, be willing to get up quickly, dust yourself off, and move forward. Resist the temptation to throw a self-pity party and get stuck at your lowest points in life. Resist the temptation to sweep it under the rug and try to hide it, since God knows anyway. Make the choice to get past your mistakes as quickly as you can. Be willing to take personal responsibility and deal with them rather than blame everyone else, including God, for your problems. To help with this, find an accountability partner. Make sure it's someone you trust that can keep you honest. Make sure they have your best interest at heart and can encourage you. You not only have to be able to talk with them about anything, but you must be willing to listen to what they have to say. It may be your spouse, or it may be a close friend. The freedom to forgive (yourself and others) comes with the knowledge that you are accepted in the eyes of God for who you are, not who you can be.

Always remember that who you *are* is more important than what you *do*. In America, we seem to have that backwards. When you meet someone for the first time, one of the first questions asked is usually, "What do you do?" You size up the person by their response. You develop some opinions of them based on their answer to that one simple question. So, how do you know who you are? Who you are is determined by your character. Your character is shaped by your choices. Your choices are ultimately determined by your faith. The problem is that much of this struggle is undetectable by anyone outside of ourself. Much of the struggle with character-shaping decisions happens when no one else is looking. When you notice you are living one way for everyone to see and another way when no one is watching (except God, of course), *watch out!* Use your journaling and accountability partner as a sounding board to get through these struggles. You can do it!

You are responsible for your own relationship with God. It's not your pastor's job to develop you spiritually. The main function of the church is to win and disciple the lost. Most churches spend too much time just trying to keep a bunch of Christians happy. That may be an eye-opener to some of you. Whether your church has forty or forty-thousand, you can't place the weight of your spiritual growth on someone else. Don't get me wrong, you can learn from and be taught by someone else, but the responsibility to grow is on you. Many think church is where they go to sit and be fed. We do receive teaching, encouragement, and spiritual nourishment from our church and pastors, but too many believe it's the pastor's job (what they *pay* him to do) to make them a better Christian. They show up each week, expecting enough spiritual food to last them until the next weekend. During the week, spiritual growth is ignored, since it's not their responsibility. It has been God's desire since the beginning of time to build a relationship of closeness and intimacy with you personally, so make it a priority to spend time with God on your own. To help you in this area, get plugged into some sort of ministry in your church. Get involved in serving instead of just showing up. Find a spiritual mentor, someone that is further along in their relationship with God than you are. Spend time with them, learn from them, and glean from their experience. Better yet, become a spiritual mentor to someone not as far as you in their relationship with God. If you do not fast regularly, integrate it into your life as a regular spiritual discipline. All these things will help you maintain a healthy relationship with God and push you forward.

God knows what is best for you. Do you believe that? If you do, then in the midst of difficulty or frustration, don't rashly make choices to try and remove yourself from difficult situation. When you do, you may be making a mistake. Even worse, you may actually be deciding that you know what is best for your own life! Of course, by making that decision, you are also letting God know you don't think He knows what He is doing! Remember that patience is a virtue, but impatience is a curse. It took Noah over one hundred years to build the ark before there was even one drop of rain. Sarah was ninety years old before she gave birth to a son. Things will not always happen *when* or *how* you want them to. When you feel the frustration of your circumstances is beginning to overwhelm you, journal about your thoughts and feelings to help you process them. Use your accountability partner to talk through things. Listen to what the people that have earned the right to speak into your life have to say, then look to God for answers and wait patiently.

Spiritual apathy will make you content with where you are in your relationship with God. Sometimes a disappointing situation or set of circumstances will cause us to *give up* on our relationship with God in some way. It can happen in any relationship. Think about marriage. On the day of your wedding, while reciting your vows and looking into the eyes of your soon-to-be spouse, you were (or will be) overwhelmed with feelings of love. You don't maintain that emotional high for the rest of your marriage. You settle into the everyday routine, and before you know it, you begin to take your relationship with your spouse for granted. You don't love your spouse any less than the day you married them, but you don't *feel* those same feelings all the time.

Guard yourself against allowing your feelings to dictate your relationship with God. The emotional intensity that accompanies our feelings and experiences will come and go. One of the greatest misunderstandings of modern-day Christianity is the belief that Christians are supposed to be happy all the time. That is just not true, much less realistic. You have the right to be sad, mad, frustrated, and all the other things that come with life! We were created to experience a full range of emotions that extends to both ends of the spectrum. Happiness is just one of those feelings, but it is based solely on our situation or circumstances. Because life is hard at times, we will not always be happy. Joy is more than a feeling. To the Christian, it's an understanding; contentment because of the knowledge of what the future holds. It's why, even in the midst of difficult circumstances and a variety of emotions, you can have joy. Just like your relationship with your spouse takes work, so does your relationship with God. We cannot allow our feelings to dictate our relationship with God! We cannot serve God only when we feel like it. We have to wake up, open our eyes, and get going!

AUTHOR CONTACT

If you enjoyed *Wake Up America,* author Steve Strickland may be available to speak at your next event. Steve is a gifted teacher and dynamic communicator of God's Word. Questions, comments, or inquiries can be directed to: steve.diane@juno.com, or on his blog at: stevestrickland.blogspot.com

ENDNOTES

1. 49 Million Born Again Adults Shared Their Faith in Jesus in the Past Year, July 23, 2003 (www.barna.org)

2. "Benjamin: Son of the Right Hand," New Era, May 1974, pg. 34–37

3. W. Phillip Keller, "Joshua, Mighty Warrior and Man of Faith", pg. 179

4. Keller, pg. 160–161

5. http://www.miami.com/mld/miamiherald/entertainment/8829344.htm?1c

6. http://www.apologeticsindex.org/d50.html

7. http://www.amazon.com/exec/obidos/tg/detail/-/0786868716/104–7501455–6435131?v=glance&s=books&vi=reviews

8. http://www.usatoday.com/life/books/news/2004–03–10-bookslist-decade-main_x.htm

9. Warren Wiersbe, "The Bible Exposition Commentary"

10. Barna Lists the 12 Most Significant Religious Findings from 2006 Surveys, December 20, 2006, (www.barna.org)

11. Surveys Show Pastors Claim Congregants Are Deeply Committed to God But Congregants Deny It!, January 10, 2006, (www.barna.org)

12. The Concept of Holiness Baffles Most Americans, February 20, 2006, (www.barna.org)

13. Gene Edwards, "A Tale of Three Kings", p. 17–20

14. Ted Haggard, "Primary Purpose", p. 109

15. http://bible1.crosswalk.com/Lexicons/Greek/grk.cgi?number=5273&version=KJV

16. http://en.wikipedia.org/wiki/The_Picture_of_Dorian_Gray

17. Quoted by Dr. Curt Watke, Director of Kim School of Multi-cultural Studies, Golden Gate Theological Seminary, January 28, 2003, Readiness Retreat, Amicalola Falls, Ga.

18. Van Sanders, Calling Out the Called, Empowering Believers To Impact Their Community. (Alpharetta, Ga.: North American Mission Board, SBC, Alpharetta, GA, 2001), p.2.